Contents

Acknowledgements

This project has relied heavily on the goodwill of large numbers of people. We are indebted to the people with learning difficulties and practitioners who took part in the work at each of the five sites. The project would not have existed without their involvement, input, time, energy and enthusiasm.

Others who deserve our thanks include Alex O'Neil and Linda Ward from the Joseph Rowntree Foundation, for their support and encouragement; Jane Charlton and Karen Gyde (Norah Fry Research Centre), for their willing, interested and conscientious administrative support; Beth Prewett, Jane Eccles and Pat Simmons who proofread and edited an early draft of the report; Chris Gaine, Joyce Kallevic and Emma King from ERAS who assisted with fieldwork; and Pam Townsley for reading and amending the final proofs.

We were fortunate to have access to two separate advisory groups who offered expertise and support in a number of practical ways (see Appendix A). Many thanks to Liz Billinghurst, Richard Bowerman, Paul Clarke, Colin Evans, Kerrie Ford, Rosemary Gammon, Monica Holly, Jane Livingston, Geoff Marks, Kim Norman, Hilary Simpson, Naomi Thomas, and Keith Walker.

Finally our thanks must go to the Joseph Rowntree Foundation for funding the project, and for offering additional support in helping us to resolve some of the many practical and methodological issues that arose throughout the work.

Summary

About the report

This report describes and reflects upon the process of working with five sites to improve practice and promote change in one specific area – user involvement in staff recruitment. The 'Learning to choose staff' project worked with five organisations providing services to people with learning difficulties in England. Drawing on evidence from our previous research (Townsley and Macadam, 1996; Townsley et al, 1997), we set up a training and development programme designed to promote and support the involvement of people with learning difficulties in staff recruitment. We evaluated the process by collecting data from project participants (including ourselves as members of the project team).

This report describes the main steps involved in our work with sites. We look at what happened when we brought people together and how we enabled the sites to reflect on their own practice. We discuss how we supported sites to learn about user involvement in recruitment, and evaluated the progress made by project participants in developing and sustaining their own initiatives. The report concludes with a summary of strategies for promoting change and improving practice, with reference to the evidence-base provided by the work of the 'Learning to choose staff' project. All identifying characteristics of people, organisations and geographical areas has been changed.

Who is the report for?

This report is aimed at practitioners, managers and policy makers working in services for people with learning difficulties. It will be of primary interest to those wishing to involve people with learning difficulties in recruiting new staff.

The report will also be of interest to those wishing to work in partnership with other professionals and/or people with learning difficulties to achieve a particular goal or outcome.

Both the model of the project itself and the strategies developed by participants could inform a wide range of other projects or initiatives where the aim is to promote change and improve practice.

Main messages

- The work with sites followed four main steps:
  (1) bringing people together;
  (2) reflecting on current practice;
  (3) learning and planning; and
  (4) developing, supporting and evaluating initiatives.

- At each of the four steps, the project team disseminated key findings about the value of involving people with learning difficulties in staff recruitment. They also provided opportunities for participants to practise skills, learn and work together, and evaluate their own practice and progress. The participation of people with learning difficulties at each step, and the co-learning model adopted during the training programme (step 3), allowed the team to model good practice in user involvement throughout the project.

- Evidence from the project demonstrated that the structure of the four-step model was a crucial factor in enabling participants to develop successful initiatives. The combination of opportunities to meet, talk, learn, practise, reflect and assess enabled some participants to make significant changes to their policy and practice. By the end of the project, four of the five sites had developed detailed plans for initiatives to promote user involvement in staff recruitment, and three sites had implemented their plans at policy and/or practice level.

- Project participants used a number of different strategies to promote, change and develop practice and policy relating to user involvement in choosing staff. These strategies fell into five areas: commitment and attitudes; working together; organising resources; developing skills and knowledge; evaluating the process.

- Strategies for generating and maintaining commitment were fundamental to developing initiatives to promote user involvement in recruitment. When commitment was lost, challenged or eroded, even the most well planned initiatives were unable to flourish.

'How to choose staff'

'How to choose staff' is an audio-tape and accompanying booklet for people with learning difficulties. Produced in the style of a radio programme, the tape summarises the work of the 'Learning to choose staff' project and the main messages for people with learning difficulties. The tape was made by a group of people with learning difficulties who acted as advisers to the project team.

You can get a copy from Marston Book Services, PO Box 269, Abingdon, OX14 4YN; tel 01235 465 538. The pack is free to individual self-advocates and service user groups. The ISBN is 1 86134 450 3.

Learning to choose staff: a project to promote change and improve practice

Promoting change

In 1996 the Joseph Rowntree Foundation set up a new funding programme to support work that aimed to 'promote change and improve practice'. The Foundation was aware that research findings alone are not always the most effective way of influencing practice. It is all too easy for busy practitioners to be unaware of, or to ignore, recommendations for good practice, even when these are well publicised and available in user-friendly formats (Kirk, 1996). For research to have any significant impact, it is necessary to find ways to encourage and support practitioners to put research into action.

The 'Learning to choose staff' project

The 'Learning to choose staff' project put research findings directly into the hands of professionals and people with learning difficulties. We used good practice recommendations drawn from our previous research in the area of user involvement in staff recruitment as the basis for setting up an initiative designed to promote and stimulate change. We worked with five sites in England, all

of whom were providing services to people with learning difficulties. We offered a training programme, supported the development work of the sites, and evaluated the success of the process, both in terms of its impact on the practice of the sites and as a model for promoting change and improving practice more widely.

Involving people with learning difficulties in staff recruitment – a prime area for promoting change and improving practice

Our previous research in this area (Townsley and Macadam, 1996) had already identified a number of factors that promoted and inhibited effective user involvement in the recruitment process. One of the main issues identified was the importance of training and support. Where this was available, people with learning difficulties were far more likely to participate fully and effectively in the decision-making process about whom to appoint to work with them. The provision of such training and support also helped to allay the concerns of practitioners that people with learning difficulties did not have the necessary skills to take part in selecting staff.

Very few services, however, had developed or implemented such training for professionals or people with learning difficulties. Practitioners cited the lack of published training materials specifically available for people with learning difficulties as a barrier to setting up training. More worryingly, we found that in some places, people were expected to participate in staff recruitment having received little or no training. One research respondent neatly summed up the problems associated with this:

> "We can't throw people with learning difficulties into a situation like recruitment without giving them all the training, support and practice they need. I myself find the interview process very nerve racking. I've only learnt how to cope through having training."
> (Support worker, local authority day service, quoted in Townsley and Macadam, 1996, p 73)

In response to these findings, we produced a resource pack aimed at trainers and supporters working with people with learning difficulties (Townsley et al, 1997). The pack takes the reader through all the main stages involved in the process of staff recruitment and makes recommendations for good practice drawn from the research evidence presented in its companion research report (Townsley and Macadam, 1996).

Our knowledge that documents alone do not promote change was the basis for the 'Learning to choose staff' project. Our previous research had highlighted the need for training and we had duly

produced a pack to meet this need. However, the next step was to find out what happens when professionals and people with learning difficulties are actively encouraged to put these ideas into practice. What new barriers might they come up against? What extra support and information might they need?

About this report

This report describes and evaluates the process of working with five sites to improve practice and promote change in one specific area – user involvement in staff recruitment. Chapter 2 outlines the model of good practice in recruitment that informed the development of work with sites. Chapter 3 introduces the sites themselves, summarises the four main steps of the training and development programme, and explains how we evaluated the progress of the work while documenting participants' reactions, successes and difficulties. Chapters 4, 5, 6 and 7 then take each of the four main steps in turn and draw out key themes for promoting change and improving practice. Chapter 4 focuses on what happened when we brought people together. Chapter 5 looks at how we enabled the sites to reflect on their own current practice. Chapter 6 shows how we supported sites to learn about user involvement in recruitment and to plan for the next stage of the project. Chapter 7 discusses the progress made by project participants and the impact of developing, supporting and evaluating the different initiatives. Finally, Chapter 8 concludes with a summary of strategies for promoting change and improving practice, with reference to the evidence base provided by the work of the 'Learning to choose staff' project.

Good practice in involving people with learning difficulties in recruiting staff

In order to bring about changes and improvements to services and support it is necessary to have in mind some concept of what good, or better, practice might look like. Our previous research (Townsley and Macadam, 1996; Townsley et al, 1997) had already highlighted a range of important and salient issues. We re-examined this literature in order to tease out key evidence about what works in implementing user involvement in recruitment. This chapter outlines the main recommendations for good practice in involving people with learning difficulties in recruiting staff.

Getting commitment to the concepts

The first step towards implementing successful involvement is to establish commitment to the main concepts. This includes commitment from people with learning difficulties, policy makers, managers and support staff to the idea and ethos of user involvement in the recruitment process, and an acknowledgement of the likely benefits. Each of these groups should have thought through the question 'why involve?' and be prepared to champion the cause of

user involvement if met with objections. Implicit here is a commitment to working together, across practitioner and service user boundaries, in order to achieve change. In practice this might involve joint meetings, or training sessions.

It is important for people with learning difficulties to decide how they want to be involved in the recruitment process, or indeed if they wish to be involved at all. Commitment from people with learning difficulties is a basic and vital ingredient of successful involvement. But our research showed that commitment to the idea of user involvement is best developed where people with learning difficulties have chances to learn and practise skills and where their views are valued by staff.

Commitment to involvement throughout the whole recruitment process is also key. Recruitment is not just about interviewing, it is a process which includes a range of activities:

- drawing up a person specification and job description;
- advertising the post;
- making an information pack;
- drawing up an application form;

- shortlisting candidates;
- planning the interview day;
- making a list of questions to ask;
- conducting a formal interview;
- organising other formal activities designed to elicit information about candidates' skills, knowledge and attitudes;
- devising an assessment tool;
- assessing or scoring candidates;
- making the final decision;
- informing candidates of the outcome.

Where people with learning difficulties are involved at every stage, the outcomes are likely to be more positive for everyone concerned. This is particularly true when people with learning difficulties are involved in drawing up a person specification. If they are clear about the sort of person needed from the outset, the whole recruitment process makes more sense and is easier to understand for everyone. However, it is important to be realistic about what can be achieved straightaway. Learning to recruit staff is a complex process and requires learning and practising a set of skills that will be new to most people with learning difficulties. It is important to start with small steps, whilst keeping in mind the goal of full involvement at every stage. Successful involvement means supporting people with learning difficulties to design a format that is enjoyable for them and involves them in the most meaningful way possible. This may mean starting with a very basic level of involvement and moving on to other levels as and when people feel confident to do so. People should not be forced into participating in, for example, formal interviewing, if they do not feel comfortable with this.

Commitment, by managers and policy makers, to providing adequate resources

for training and support is central to the successful implementation of user involvement in recruitment. It is irresponsible if services expect people with learning difficulties to take part in a process as complex and demanding as recruitment without access to good training and support.

Planning the process

Once there is a commitment to the underlying concepts, the next steps involve building an infrastructure of support, training, resources and networks in readiness for putting user involvement in recruitment into practice.

Liaison and collaboration with trade unions and personnel departments is very important at this stage. These professionals will want to be involved, or at the very least, kept informed. Liaison should involve finding out about any established procedures, such as the way in which posts are advertised. It may be helpful also to invite them to play a role in training, or to meet the people with learning difficulties who are involved in the initiative. Most personnel departments need to ensure that any involvement is following equal opportunities and fair selection guidelines. Encouraging them to join in the training, or be part of the involvement process may help to alleviate any concerns they may have. Providing feedback after the recruitment process is also an effective way to keep trades union and personnel staff informed.

Networking and exchanging information with other people and organisations is an important way of finding out more about how to implement user involvement in recruitment. The awareness that user involvement is going on elsewhere may also be a strong motivating factor for many managers and policy makers!

The importance of providing good training and support has already been highlighted in Chapter 1. The role of a supporter of people with learning difficulties should include:

- setting up opportunities for training, practice and preparation;
- assisting with reading, writing, speaking or other communication;
- translating, communicating or advocating on behalf of people with complex support needs;
- helping with practical details;
- facilitating the interview, or other recruitment activity, and supporting people to ask questions and give their views;
- liaising with other relevant professionals.

Supporters should have already received some training in the recruitment process themselves, or at the very least, be familiar with the stages of the process. It is probably easiest and best if the supporter also conducts the training for people with learning difficulties, although the value of bringing in an independent facilitator could also be considered.

The funding and delivery of recruitment training may well require some time to arrange, so should be considered well in advance of the proposed involvement. Training for people with learning difficulties should:

- cover the whole recruitment process;
- address equal opportunities and confidentiality;
- use accessible materials;

- involve a trainer who is knowledgeable about the recruitment process.

Putting it into practice

This is the point at which people with learning difficulties are able to get involved in recruiting staff. Considerations at this stage involve implementing the details of the actual recruitment process and involvement in this. We have already discussed the importance of understanding that the recruitment process has many stages, and of aiming for involvement in all of these. Again, ensuring that people with learning difficulties are involved at the stage of drawing up a person specification is key, even if involvement at subsequent stages is less developed to begin with (Howarth et al, 2000).

The level of posts in which people are involved also needs to be discussed at this stage. As a baseline, people with learning difficulties should start by being involved in recruiting for all types of job where staff have daily, direct contact with them, or responsibility for aspects of the service that affect them. This might involve posts such as group worker, support worker, care worker, deputy manager, manager, secretary/clerical worker, caretaker, cleaner, driver or escort.

Once people have had experience of recruiting for daily, direct contact posts they might want to push for involvement in some less frequent direct contact, or infrequent contact posts. Jobs where workers have some direct contact (but not necessarily daily contact) with people with learning difficulties include psychologist, psychiatrist, area manager/team leader, social worker and so on. Posts where workers have infrequent, if any, direct contact with people with learning difficulties include finance staff, planning officer, health and safety staff, chief executive, personnel staff, computer staff and so on.

The main stages of the recruitment process are outlined above. This process might include activities that are specifically designed to elicit information about candidates' skills, knowledge and attitudes via a scored, work-related task, such as sharing a meal, or spending an evening with people with learning difficulties. Our earlier research showed that, in some places, these activities are treated in an 'informal' way. This may mean that those involved (candidates and people with learning difficulties) are unclear or unaware that the activity is actually part of the recruitment process. This is not good practice and is not a form of involvement in recruitment that we would endorse. However, scoring or assessing people during an informal activity, with their full knowledge and using agreed questions, can be very helpful. Similarly, other informal activities that do not involve questioning or assessing candidates (such as showing candidates around the service) may be useful as an ice-breaker. But these should not be scored, nor carried out by those who are also doing the formal interview.

The idea of scoring, or assessing, candidates on agreed criteria, developed from the person specification and interview questions, is central to a fair and effective recruitment process. Giving candidates a concrete assessment in terms of a numerical score provides a means to reach a quick and effective decision – the person with the highest score gets the job. Services where candidates are not scored but are assessed verbally, or

informally though discussion, report higher levels of disagreement about which candidate to appoint. Scoring also allows recruiters to find an objective way to make the final decision, and enables the views of people with learning difficulties to count in some clearly defined way.

It is important to be clear about who is ultimately responsible for the final decision, and who will have the final say in the event of any disagreement. People with learning difficulties have a right to know how much weight their decision will have, and where possible, for their input to have some direct, visible influence over the decision-making process. It is also essential to keep candidates well informed about the nature of the recruitment process and the arrangements for making the final decision. It is only fair that they should know in advance what will be involved.

Getting involved in the recruitment process will be a new activity for most people with learning difficulties. Experimenting with different ideas, finding out what works best, and being prepared to make changes if needed, are an important part of the learning process. Finally, keeping records of what happened, who was appointed and why, and any successes or problems that occurred is essential for the purposes of monitoring and feeding back to other recruiters and candidates of the outcome.

Summary

This chapter has summarised the main practice recommendations of our previous research (see also Table 1). The evidence presented indicates that successful user involvement in recruitment involves developing a number of strategies to promote and maintain commitment, to plan the process, and to put the initiative into practice. We knew that these strategies would need to be reflected in the training and development programme that we devised, and in the advice and support that we offered to the five sites involved.

Table 1: Recommendations for good practice in involving people with learning difficulties in recruitment

Getting commitment	Planning the process	Putting it into practice
To the concept of user involvement in recruitment – from people with learning difficulties, policy makers, managers and support staff	Involve trades unions	Aim for involvement at all stages of the recruitment process, but be realistic to begin with
To involvement throughout the whole recruitment process	Involve the personnel department	Ensure that people with learning difficulties are involved right from the start
To working together across staff and service user boundaries	Network and exchange information	Aim for involvement in recruitment for all posts, but start with daily direct contact posts
To providing resources for adequate training and support	Get resources	Avoid making informal activities part of the recruitment process
	Provide support	Keep candidates informed
	Provide training	Find an objective way to make the final decision
	Consider how to involve people who communicate non-verbally	Be clear about the extent of influence by people with learning difficulties over the final decision
	Become familiar with the recruitment process	Be prepared to experiment and make changes
	Provide opportunities for practice	Monitor, record and evaluate the process
	Provide clear, written practice guidance and / or policy guidelines	

3

A training and development programme for learning to choose staff

Chapter 2 described the model of good practice underlying our work on the 'Learning to choose staff' project. This model informed the development of the programme of work that we devised and the advice and support that we offered to the five sites. Chapter 3 introduces the five sites, summarises the four main steps of the training and development programme, and explains how we evaluated the progress of the work while documenting participants' reactions, successes and difficulties.

The five sites

The first task was to negotiate access with five sites which provided services to people with learning difficulties in England. This number was chosen to allow for a sufficient range of services while keeping the project on a manageable scale, and included residential and day services from the voluntary, statutory and private sectors, representing small, medium, large and national organisations.

The five sites that took part in the project were:

1. **Attingham City Council** – a large, local, statutory provider of day services
2. **Bradworth Care Trust** – a large, local, voluntary provider of residential and supported living services
3. **Cherry Tree House** – a medium, local, private provider of residential and day services
4. **Danbury House** – a small, local, private provider of residential services
5. **Edgehill Housing Association** – a large, national, voluntary provider of residential and supported living services.

Attingham City Council

Attingham City Council provided day services to 720 adults with learning difficulties. At the time of the site's involvement in the project, people with learning difficulties accessed the service via staffed centres, or units. Each centre had its own staff group and manager. The centre managers reported to a team leader, who in turn was overseen by a service manager. Practitioners within the service were employed by the local authority and were therefore subject to that organisation's policies and procedures. Any changes to official policies or procedures were submitted to the appropriate corporate committee (for example, social services committee, corporate services committee), who would take the decision as to whether such changes were warranted. Organisational change was thus a lengthy and rather bureaucratic process, and one that the 'Learning to choose staff' project would find it difficult to influence directly. A draft policy, written in 1996, existed on 'Service user involvement in staff selection within day provision', but had not been implemented. It was suggested to us that this had been put 'on hold' pending the results of the involvement by the services in the 'Learning to choose staff' project.

Bradworth Care Trust

Bradworth Care Trust was a provider of residential care and supported living services to people with learning difficulties and people with mental health care needs. 154 people with learning difficulties lived in 31 staffed homes and supported living units. Each house had a home manager, and each supported living service was overseen by a coordinator. These services were managed by a number of community managers, who were in turn responsible to a service development manager and head of learning difficulties services. Overall responsibility for financial issues and policy decisions rested with a Board, consisting of a number of trustees, the chief executive, and members of the senior management team.

Cherry Tree House

Cherry Tree House consisted of three houses and a day centre providing residential and day services to people

with learning difficulties. Residents and staff from two of the houses took part in the 'Learning to choose staff' project. Of these, one house accommodated 32 residents in three units, while the other was registered for eight people. There were 25 members of full- and part-time staff working at the two houses. Although each part of the service had its own manager (of whom two were involved in the project), the overall responsibility for the development of the service rested with the owner/proprietor.

Danbury House

Danbury House provided residential services to 12 people with learning difficulties. There were 11 members of staff (five full-time, five part-time), including the manager. Four new part-time staff had very recently been appointed – residents were involved informally in this (as discussed later).

Danbury House was a charity and was overseen by four Trustees who had decision-making powers, but who had devolved responsibility for care and management issues to the home manager. The Trustees were not involved in staff recruitment, and Danbury House had not yet developed a written recruitment policy, although plans were in place to draft this.

Edgehill Housing Association

Edgehill Housing Association, a national organisation, provided residential services to people with learning difficulties and people with mental health care needs. We worked with people with learning difficulties, support staff and home managers from one regional area, and with policy makers from across the organisation as a whole. Within the local area involved in the project, there were six staffed houses, one supported living service, and a short breaks service. These units provided accommodation for 32 tenants with learning difficulties and short break services to another 30 people with learning difficulties. Each house, or unit, had its own home manager, who reported to the local area manager.

Our key contact locally was the service development manager who, together with the regional manager, was responsible for area/regional policy and operational issues. Overall, the organisation was managed by a chief executive (based in a city in another region) and overseen by a board of trustees.

The four main steps of 'Learning to choose staff'

The programme of work with each of the five sites followed a four-step format:

1. Bringing people together
2. Reflecting on current practice
3. Learning and planning
4. Developing, supporting and evaluating initiatives.

At each of the four steps, the project team disseminated key findings about the value of involving people with learning difficulties in recruitment. We also provided opportunities for participants to practise skills, learn and work together, and evaluate their own practice and progress. More details of the work conducted by the project team and participants at each step will be described in Chapters 4 to 7.

Supporting people to work together across boundaries

Sloper et al (1999) explain that initiatives to promote change and improve practice require complex changes, both for individuals and for their organisations. We recognised that this would be true for the sites with whom we were hoping to work. Our previous research had highlighted that user involvement in recruitment requires practitioners and service users to work together and to share ideas. It also requires significant commitment to the concept of user participation in service development, and a willingness (by practitioners) to 'let go' of traditional practices and boundaries.

Figure 1 shows the extent of the cooperation and collaboration needed between the four groups whom we hoped to involve in the project at each of the five sites.

In order to support people to work together across boundaries, we knew that the four main steps of the project would also need to model good practice in cooperative and collaborative behaviours.

Researching and analysing our work with sites

The 'Learning to choose staff' project was not just a training and development project. We also aimed to research the process of our work with sites by evaluating the progress of the work and documenting participants' reactions, successes and difficulties. To achieve this, we collected research data throughout the project from three sources:

Figure 1: Cooperation required for the successful development of user involvement in staff recruitment

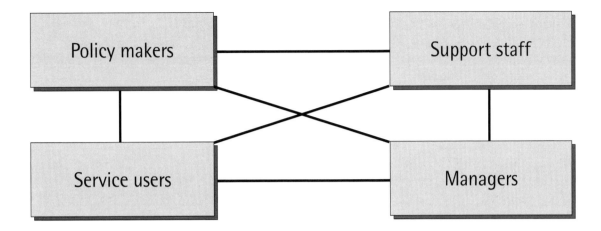

1. **Practitioners** – pre-training interview data; training notes; training evaluation forms; final interview data; minutes of all meetings; associated materials, documents and policies
2. **People with learning difficulties** – pre-training interview data; training notes; training evaluation interview data; final interview data; associated materials and documents
3. **The project team** – training de-brief; training notes; research diary and fieldwork notes; minutes of the regular progress meetings held by the project team.

The project team comprised four people, each taking a different role. Ruth Townsley, a researcher, was responsible for the overall project design, development work with sites and the evaluation. Joyce Howarth and Mark Graham, as trainers, took on the planning and implementation of the training programme and also undertook some development work with sites. Peter LeGrys, a consultant on service user involvement, supported the Service User Advisory Group (see Appendix A) and offered advice to the project team on

good practice in user involvement more generally.

As the list above indicates, collecting data from ourselves as members of the project team was as important to us as collecting data from the project participants. We also viewed ourselves as participants in the work, and were aware that our actions and interventions were part of the research and development process and so worthy of scrutiny and analysis. In this way, the planning and development of initiatives at each site was very much a group process between the project team and project participants. Data about our role in this process will thus be examined alongside other data collected throughout the project.

We hoped that the range and depth of data we collected along the way would enable us to shed some light on how promoting change and improving practice might be achieved in a project of this nature. The next four chapters take each of the main steps in turn and draw out the key themes that emerged as we supported and encouraged the sites to learn to choose staff.

4

Bringing people together

The first step of the work was to bring people together to discuss the scope and nature of the 'Learning to choose staff' project and their involvement in it. Our objectives at this stage were thus to:

- make contact and meet with key people;
- get commitment to the project;
- keep the views of people with learning difficulties at the forefront;
- document agreement to take part;
- sort out practical arrangements for the next step of the work;
- provide information about the project as a whole and respond to any immediate queries or issues.

We did this by setting up a series of introductory meetings and presentations at each site which focused on the following issues:

- why involve? – the benefits of user involvement in recruitment;
- stages of the recruitment process – it is not just about doing interviews;
- the main stages of the 'Learning to choose staff' project and the likely time commitment needed;
- participants' expectations of the project and if or how these would be met;

- discussion of how the format of the training and development might be changed to fit any particular needs;
- brief discussion of the nature and extent of current user involvement of sites in staff recruitment, including any current opportunities and obstacles;
- importance of endorsement of the project from the personnel department and trade unions;
- practical arrangements for the pre-training audit (see Chapter 5) and the training days;
- identification of key contacts at each site;
- provision of a pack of background information – project leaflet, articles, reading list, details of training programme.

We took written notes during meetings with sites and these were typed up and fed back to those involved.

This chapter discusses how the work conducted by the project team and participants at this stage started to bring about changes and improvements in practice at each site.

Beginning to work together

Bringing people together was, in itself, an important opportunity for participants at each site to establish relationships and begin to work together, often for the very first time. It was also an essential part of building relationships, and trust, between the project team members and project participants.

Identifying key contacts

In order to find a 'way in', we identified a 'key contact' person at each site. We did this either via existing personal links with these organisations, or by simply 'cold-calling' the service and speaking with the most senior person available on that particular day. In three of the sites we had just one key contact, but in the remaining two we maintained contact with several key people throughout the project. Maintaining contact with several key people appeared to work well in this context, but was probably facilitated by the small scale of these two services and could be difficult to maintain with larger organisations.

Identifying other project participants and getting their agreement to take part

In all the sites, we worked together with our key contact person to decide who should take part in the project and how participants should be recruited. We agreed that key contacts would nominate other professionals whom they felt should be included in the project. In the main this was unproblematic – it was usually quite obvious which practitioners were needed from each of the stakeholder groups and the key contacts were usually in agreement with this. However, during our meetings at one site, we had to make a strong case for including representatives from the Personnel Department and Unions, since our key contact person had advised us that his manager wanted to keep Personnel and the Unions informed of the project, rather than directly involved in it. We pointed out the importance of keeping these two groups of practitioners involved, and explained that this aspect of the project was not negotiable.

Recruiting people with learning difficulties to the project was carried out through introductory meetings and presentations at the sites. We left consent forms and project leaflets which people then returned to us if they wished to take part. Involvement in the project was therefore self-selecting for people with learning difficulties, and on a first come, first served basis. In all of the sites this appeared to be an effective way of recruiting people with learning difficulties to the project.

The need for close joint working with key contacts

We found that we relied heavily on the cooperation and support of our key contacts at each site. We needed their help not only to identify other participants, but also to highlight any potentially sensitive issues of which we needed to be aware. All our key contacts were committed to the ethos of the project. Several people spent a great deal of time and effort raising awareness of the existence of the project among practitioners and people with learning difficulties and getting agreement from these people to take part.

In one site, however, we experienced problems due to the fact that our key contact was acting in lieu of the Director of Social Services. This Director was not involved directly in the project, but nevertheless wished to pass on her views about how the project should be implemented in his service. Although we felt strongly that these views were different from those held by the project team, it was difficult to counter them directly, since they were given to us 'second-hand'. We achieved a resolution by having a frank and honest discussion about the scope of the project with our key contact and two other senior staff members. Although this felt hard at the time, it did help to clarify some of the issues that had been difficult to address in earlier meetings.

Building commitment

We were aware that in bringing people together we would need to support participants at each site to establish commitment to the main concepts. This included commitment from people with learning difficulties, policy makers, managers and support staff to the idea and ethos of user involvement in the recruitment process, and an acknowledgement of the likely benefits. Some sites needed more input on the benefits of user involvement in recruitment, while others were already committed to the concept and needed no extra persuasion by us.

Developing champions

All our key contact people showed great interest in the 'Learning to choose staff' project and were committed to the concept of involving people with learning difficulties in the recruitment process. In two sites, the key contacts also became 'champions' for the project, in that they took a great deal of personal responsibility for urging other

practitioners within their organisation/ service to consider the importance of user involvement.

Defining commitment

It was also at this stage that people began to discuss their understanding of how user involvement in recruitment might work in practice and thus to define the extent and nature of their commitment to the process.

For Attingham City Council, the definition of what constituted user involvement in recruitment was the subject of some debate during several of the introductory meetings. This site, perhaps because of its size and complexity, found it hard to commit to a model of user involvement in recruitment where people with learning difficulties played a role in the decision-making process about whom to appoint. People with learning difficulties themselves wanted full involvement, including a say in the decision-making process. Indeed they suggested that they may well refuse to take part in any moves to involve them in the recruitment process if their views about who should get the job did not count in some concrete way. The majority of support staff and managers also subscribed to this viewpoint. Among policy makers, several perceptions of what constituted a model of user involvement held sway. Two of the policy makers involved in the project had in fact been responsible for writing a draft policy on 'Service User Involvement in Staff Selection within Day Provision', which advocated involvement in shortlisting, on the formal interview panel and in decision making. The draft policy also outlined a list of topics that training for people with learning difficulties should cover. However, it was a formal letter from a senior policy maker that finally spelled out how Attingham City Council would define their participation in the project:

> "We recognise your wish to extend and develop empowerment of people with learning difficulties. We must be clear that full responsibility and accountability for recruitment decisions rests with line managers. The most suitable model is 'consultation' – that is, managers should involve and consult people with learning difficulties and aim to increase common understanding. The process is not negotiation and need not result in agreement on all sides. We feel the most productive areas for service user involvement are in informal procedures (for example, contributing to information giving to candidates); planning and preparing questions; interviewing candidates. We would wish to promote service user involvement primarily in direct service jobs – day centre officers, community support workers, senior group workers and so on. We would see it as less appropriate to focus on managerial posts. It is important that service users are clear about the basis of their involvement and their rights in all processes." (Letter to the project team from a senior policy maker at Attingham City Council, 19 November 1998)

Clearly the definition above was at odds with our understanding of how sites were to be involved in the project, and we were disappointed that the aims of the project were to be diluted in this way. Nevertheless we felt it was important to continue to work with Attingham City

Council, since we were aware of the need to take a pragmatic approach to promoting change. We also hoped that some ground would be gained by people with learning difficulties during the training days.

The situation at Bradworth Care Trust was rather different. A formal, written policy existed which had been developed by our key contact, the Service Development Manager. This policy stated, quite unequivocally, that:

> "From 1 January 1998 people with learning difficulties will be involved in the recruitment and selection of staff for the home where they live. Homes' staff will support people with learning difficulties to understand and take part in the selection and recruitment process as part of their ongoing work about rights and responsibility so that they will feel prepared when a vacancy arises." (Bradworth Care Trust's policy on 'Involving Users in the Recruitment and Selection of Staff', 1997)

The policy also clarified Bradworth Care Trust's model of user involvement in recruitment, which clearly reflected the principles underlying the 'Learning to choose staff' project. It advocated involvement at all stages of the process, with particular emphasis on drawing up a person specification. The policy was supplemented by a training manual which covered the main steps of the recruitment process, and drew heavily on our own resource pack (Townsley et al, 1997).

For Edgehill Housing Association, our key contact was equally enthusiastic about the concept of user involvement and in his organisation's participation in the project.

Despite the fact that no formal, written policy existed, the ethos of user involvement was very much in evidence during meetings and conversations with policy makers and managers at Edgehill Housing Association. A draft policy relating to tenant participation across the service summed up this approach:

> "[Edgehill Housing Association] wishes to encourage the participation of tenants in the way in which services and housing are provided and the way in which decisions are made. Our aim is to be an organisation which is open, flexible and accessible to tenants and people with learning difficulties." (Edgehill Housing Association's draft 'Tenant Participation Strategy', 1997)

Cherry Tree House and Danbury House had fewer preconceptions about how user involvement in recruitment might operate in their services, mainly because this was not something either staff or people with learning difficulties there had really considered in any depth. There was therefore less conflict between participants at this stage, and a general willingness to get involved in the project 'and just see what it was all about'. This seems to indicate that defining commitment can sometimes be easier when everyone is starting from scratch together.

Encountering different levels of commitment

Although our key contact people were committed to the concepts underlying the project, we soon found that this commitment was not necessarily endorsed by other people whose support was

nonetheless important to getting the project off the ground at each site.

Our introductory meetings and presentations at Attingham City Council highlighted a certain amount of disjunction between the views of key people (such as between managers and policy makers) and indeed between our key contact and the project team. Attingham City Council already had some experience of involving people with learning difficulties in recruitment, which was largely the result of pressure from people with learning difficulties themselves. As a large and highly structured organisation, they perceived their involvement in the 'Learning to choose staff' project as pilot work, the findings of which they intended to use as a rationale for increased participation potentially at a later date.

During our initial meetings with Bradworth Care Trust, it appeared that a key group of policy makers and managers were deeply committed to the concept of user involvement and highly enthusiastic about participating in the project. However, some other policy makers (the Personnel Manager and Trustees, for example) were more sceptical and were keen to emphasise the legal responsibilities that are attendant on the recruitment process. The degree of commitment from people with learning difficulties and support staff was unclear. Certainly it seemed that for Bradworth Care Trust, pressure for change was emanating from the 'top down', rather than from a grass-roots level as it had in Attingham City Council.

The introductory meetings at Edgehill Housing Association also highlighted some concerns and reservations from support staff. Staff from three houses in particular were not keen to take part in the project. Their reasons centred on their belief that the tenants whom they supported would not be able to take part either in the recruitment process itself, or in training about the recruitment process. There was some truth in this assertion. The tenants in question were people with complex support needs, most of whom communicated non-verbally. As it stood, our training programme would not have been accessible to them. However, there was no reason why these tenants could not take part in the recruitment process in some way – for example, having an input into drawing up a person specification based on their likes and dislikes, or taking part in an activity with a candidate which could be scored by staff. The challenge for the project team was to disentangle user or housing association involvement in the project from involvement in the training programme.

Our introductory work with Cherry Tree House and Danbury House was much more straightforward than that with the other sites. Since they had very little experience in user involvement, and had developed neither policies nor ideological frameworks relating to the concept of 'participation', it appeared easier to introduce our model of good practice and for this to be accepted at face value. Our impression at the early stages was that practitioners and people with learning difficulties were interested in the project, but were reserving judgement about the true value of user involvement in recruitment until after they had taken part in the training. This did not mean, however, that they were unwilling to commit themselves to the general concepts that we suggested, just that they did so more placidly and with more reservation than other sites at this stage.

Documenting commitment

We documented each site's agreement to take part in the project through written minutes of meetings and letters to participants. These documents set out the different arrangements for training and development work with each site, and acted as a 'contract' for both the sites and the project team.

Organising resources

We found that bringing people together became a much more important and time-consuming part of the project than we had foreseen. In particular, to respond to challenges as they arose and to maintain flexibility had an impact on how we organised and managed some of the practical arrangements at this stage of the project.

Responding to the advice of key contacts

We had originally thought that it might be possible to organise one introductory meeting and/or presentation per site, perhaps as a half-day event, where all stakeholders could attend and questions could be shared. However, our key contacts at the sites all felt that smaller meetings and presentations with groups of different stakeholders would be more effective. In large sites, several meetings were held with different stakeholders in different geographical areas. In smaller sites it was often possible to arrange a meeting with all the key people in one place.

The need for flexibility

As we have seen, several challenges arose during the process of bringing people together. These included disagreement between participants within a site, and disagreement between a site and the project team. Disagreement tended to occur over definition of concepts, particularly in terms of full commitment to the model of good practice that we had hoped sites would take on board. We felt that the role of the project team was to continue to promote good practice, while accepting that not all sites would be able to commit to this model fully at this early stage. We hoped that we would be able to encourage further commitment as their involvement in the project grew.

Responding to challenges

Other challenges had an impact on the planning and implementation of the project itself, such as the need to change aspects of the work or get extra input from elsewhere. The example below shows how we responded to one specific challenge that arose during our work with Edgehill Housing Association.

Earlier in this chapter we highlighted the challenge presented by support staff from Edgehill Housing Association, who felt that the people with learning difficulties they supported would not be able to be involved in the project in any way. As we saw it, the challenge for the project team was to disentangle involvement in the project from involvement in the training programme. We did not want to exclude those for whom our training was not accessible, or those staff who supported people who would not be taking part in the training. Following long discussions with our key contact person, we decided to organise some

additional days as a supplement to our 'standard' training programme. The first of these days would provide an opportunity for all staff to receive an introduction to user involvement in recruitment. Three subsequent half-days would allow one of the project team to spend time in each of the three houses where tenants were not taking part in the standard training programme. The purpose of these visits was to facilitate a discussion with staff (and tenants if possible) about possibilities for involving tenants in choosing staff. The format of these extra consultation days was kept as loose as possible to allow for insights from staff and tenants, and to ensure that we could respond to ideas and issues brought up by those involved.

As a project team, we also recognised that we needed some training ourselves on how best to support people with complex support needs to get involved in the recruitment process. We therefore commissioned an outside facilitator, with specialist skills in supporting people who communicate non-verbally, to provide us with one day's training in this area.

Developing knowledge and skills

Bringing people together was a prime opportunity for participants and project team members to begin to develop their knowledge and skills about the topic and about each other.

Sharing information about the topic

We used the introductory meetings and presentations as a means of providing participants with some basic information about the benefits of user involvement in recruitment, the main stages of the recruitment process and what involvement in the project might mean for them. This information was presented verbally, but we also left background material for participants to read at their own leisure, which included information about the commitment required of them to take part. This stage of the project was also a first chance for participants, particularly people with learning difficulties, to highlight their own experiences and share their knowledge with others.

Feedback from Bradworth Care Trust suggested that a folder might be a helpful additional resource in which to hold these materials. We produced such folders for use with Cherry Tree House, Danbury House and Edgehill Housing Association, and these were useful not only as a storage device but also as a way of maintaining the identity of the project and increasing people's awareness of it as a specific initiative.

Recognising and valuing the perspective of people with learning difficulties

In all but one site, the views and wishes of people with learning difficulties were central to our discussions with services about how best to implement the training and development programme. As already mentioned, our key contacts in Bradworth Care Trust and Edgehill Housing Association were committed to ensuring that any new initiative was grounded within the perspective of the people with learning difficulties for whom they worked. For Cherry Tree and Danbury the newness of the enterprise meant that practitioners and people with learning difficulties were learning together from the start.

At Attingham City Council, however, we did not feel that the views of people with learning difficulties were given centre stage. There is no doubt that many individual practitioners within the service were deeply committed to listening to, and respecting, the views of people with learning difficulties about how they wished to be involved in the recruitment process; and these individuals made great efforts to put forward their points of view, not only at the initial stages of the project, but also during the training programme and thereafter. However, our early discussions with Attingham City Council highlighted the fact that the views of people with learning difficulties were diluted at the point of influence. The sheer size and organisational complexity made it difficult for individual practitioners to respond quickly or flexibly to the challenges presented by user involvement in recruitment. Paradoxically, it was at this site that people with learning difficulties were most active in making their case for full and equal involvement.

Summary

This chapter has shown how the first step, of bringing people together, enabled the project team and participants to develop their practice in four key ways:

1. **Beginning to work together** – by identifying key contacts, identifying other participants, getting agreement to take part, and developing rapport and close working with key contacts

2. **Building commitment** – through key contacts as champions for the project; by defining the extent and nature of commitment, responding to different levels of commitment and by documenting commitment

3. **Organising resources** – by maintaining flexibility, responding to challenges as they arose and responding to the advice of key contacts

4. **Developing knowledge and skills** – by sharing information about the topic and by recognising and valuing one another's abilities, needs and perspectives.

In the next chapter we will examine how participants continued to develop their practice and to respond to the challenges presented by the next step of the project – reflecting on current practice.

Reflecting on current practice

Chapter 4 described the first step of bringing people together to discuss the scope and nature of the 'Learning to choose staff' project and their involvement in it. This enabled the project team and participants to make some of the practical arrangements for the next two steps of the work – reflecting on current practice, and learning and planning (to be discussed in Chapter 6).

In this chapter, we will explain the process of reflecting on current practice – through a pre-training audit and goal setting at each site – and how this helped participants to begin to make significant changes to their practice in the area of involving people with learning difficulties in staff recruitment.

Pre-training audit and goal setting

Before embarking on the training programme, we undertook an audit of current practice at each site. The audit provided a baseline with which comparison could be made at the later evaluation stages, and enabled individuals/sites to reflect on current practice and identify goals for their involvement in the project.

We documented current practice through the use of in-depth interviews with people with learning difficulties, support staff, managers and policy makers. We talked to 81 people in all – 32 people with learning difficulties, 8 support staff, 16 managers and 25 policy makers. The majority of these interviews were conducted individually; some interviews were held with groups of between two and six people. Interviews covered the following issues:

Interviews with practitioners

- individuals' roles in the recruitment process;
- existing policies – on recruitment generally, on user involvement specifically, and any others of relevance;
- current practice in relation to user involvement in recruitment;
- opportunities for promoting user involvement in recruitment – good things going on that might help the organisation to take things forward;
- obstacles – possible barriers to user involvement in recruitment;
- map of possible future involvement at each stage of the recruitment process;
- level of posts to be covered by user involvement;

- training needs of people with learning difficulties and practitioners;
- expectations of the 'Learning to choose staff' project;
- individuals' goals for taking forward user involvement in recruitment.

Interviews with people with learning difficulties

- existing involvement in choosing staff – When? At what stages of the process? Enjoyment? Problems?
- existing knowledge of the recruitment process;
- map of possible future involvement at each stage of the recruitment process.

Once we had conducted all the interviews at each site, we summarised the findings and listed the goals for each of the individuals, or groups, interviewed. These summaries were then sent to participants as a record and resource for their ongoing involvement in the project.

Evaluating practice

Our role at this stage was to conduct interviews with participants at each site and the pre-training audit did indeed highlight a range of practices across the sites. However this was a much more active process than is usual in social research of this nature. It was not simply a case of asking questions and listening to the answers. We found that the interviewer and the participant became engaged in a dialogue, or exchange of information, about the topic of user involvement in choosing staff. This process enabled participants to describe their current practice, reflect on it, and actively assess its value, often seeking additional information from members of the project team in order to do so.

Indeed the very act of responding to questions about certain aspects of that topic enabled participants to pinpoint weak or non-existent practice. In this way, the process of interviewing as part of the pre-training audit became a tool for self-reflection, and ultimately, self-evaluation.

The rest of this section summarises the pre-training practice that was in place at each site, and highlights any existing opportunities or obstacles identified by participants.

Attingham City Council

Despite the lack of any official policy or procedure, people with learning difficulties had been involved in the recruitment process at Attingham City Council for the last nine years. The extent and nature of involvement was decided on a centre-by-centre basis and was largely dependent on the interest and commitment of both the manager and people with learning difficulties at any particular unit. In the main, it appeared that involvement was restricted to the interview stage only. At some centres, people with learning difficulties were holding their own separate interviews in addition to the formal one. In other places, a service user was coopted to the formal panel. Since these procedures were not recognised officially, by the organisation as a whole or by the Personnel Department, people with learning difficulties were perceived very much as advisors, rather than equal partners, and played little direct role in the actual decision-making process. Indeed, from our initial discussions with policy makers at Attingham City Council, it appeared that the service had a clear, but rather restrictive, model of participation in mind (see Chapter 4 for more details of this).

Practitioners and people with learning difficulties used the pre-training audit as an opportunity to highlight a range of problematic issues that they wished to address:

- no recruitment training was available – yet people with learning difficulties were still encouraged to take part;
- quality of involvement varied across the different centres;
- lack of time for support and planning – in some places people were given less than one day's notice to prepare for user involvement in an interview;
- interview questions were already set by staff and were not presented in an accessible format;
- it was not clear how the views and scores of people with learning difficulties counted towards the final decision – in some centres people took part in the decision-making process, in others they did not;
- the Personnel Department's recruitment process was very complex and inaccessible to people with learning difficulties;
- no real change was possible without the agreement of the Personnel Department and the corporate services committee.

Despite these difficulties, our interviews with people with learning difficulties demonstrated a very clear commitment to continued, and increased, involvement in the recruitment of staff. In particular, people were very interested and keen to take part in the 'Learning to choose staff' training programme. As one service user explained:

"We've been asking for this course for a long time."

Bradworth Care Trust

Despite the fact that Bradworth Care Trust had a written policy stating that 'people with learning difficulties will be involved in the recruitment and selection of staff', this was not happening in all staffed houses. Where user involvement was happening, many different practices existed. These ranged from people with learning difficulties taking part in informal meetings with candidates, to the situation in one house where residents prepared a person specification, took part in the formal interview (two residents, two staff) and had an equal say in the decision-making process. The extent and nature of user involvement in recruitment at Bradworth Care Trust was thus dependent on the commitment of individual practitioners, or on pressure from people with learning difficulties.

Access to training for people with learning difficulties was patchy. The service expected each home to provide in-house training, based on the training manual that appended the policy document. However, many staff and managers felt ill-equipped to 'cascade' training in this way, and expressed a wish for the service to provide more structured learning opportunities for people with learning difficulties and support staff.

We conducted pre-training interviews with all 12 of the people with learning difficulties who had chosen to take part in the training programme. Of these, five had already been involved in recruiting staff. All were keen to learn more, or to increase their existing skills.

"I want to have more of a say – to try and see if I can do it."

"It's nice to talk to people and find out about them."

"It's important to be involved. I've not had the opportunity before."

Cherry Tree House

At the point of the pre-training audit, people with learning difficulties at Cherry Tree House were taking part in the recruitment process in an informal way only. They met and talked with candidates over a cup of tea, or an evening meal. Then the candidate was shown around the house, or spent a longer period of time taking part in a shift alongside a member of staff. A senior support worker observed the interaction between the residents and the candidate, and asked residents for their impressions of each person. The support worker then fed back their own views, and those of the residents to the home manager. The practitioners who we interviewed at Cherry Tree House admitted that it was not clear whether candidates knew they were taking part in the process of choosing staff by chatting to residents. Nor was it likely that residents were aware that these 'visitors' had come for a job interview and might be working with them in the future.

Danbury House

At Danbury House, residents were taking part in recruiting staff in an informal way. Candidates had the formal interview with the manager, followed by an opportunity to meet residents informally for a drink and a chat. The manager then talked to residents about their perceptions of each candidate. After the interview day,

successful or 'borderline' candidates were invited back to the service to spend two to three hours with residents. In the last recruitment exercise, this had taken place at a house barbecue. The purpose of the informal side of the recruitment process was for the manager to gain some extra information to supplement what candidates said in the interview. In particular, he was interested to see how candidates interacted with residents and how they treated them as people. Residents knew that the people they met had come for a job interview, but it was not clear if they understood fully that their views might count in some way towards the person getting, or not getting, the job.

We talked about the difficulties inherent in using informal processes as part of the recruitment process. Indeed the manager at Danbury House had already mentioned that he felt there was a need for residents to ask specific questions of candidates in order to identify the skills they were looking for. The idea of a separate, formal interview, by residents only, appealed to him. But he was still insistent that the informal activities played an important role in his own decision-making process about whom to appoint.

Edgehill Housing Association

At Edgehill Housing Association, people with learning difficulties were involved in the recruitment process at only one of the seven homes we visited as part of the pre-training audit. This involvement was informal only – tenants met candidates, showed them around the service, chatted to them, and fed back their views to the managers. Tenants were aware that they were taking part in the process of recruiting staff, but did not use a formal method of assessment for collating or feeding back their perceptions of candidates. In a similar way to Cherry Tree House and Danbury House, therefore, people with learning difficulties and practitioners at Edgehill Housing Association had very little prior knowledge or experience of getting involved in choosing staff.

We have already discussed the resistance that was shown towards the project by some members of support staff at Edgehill Housing Association. However, it is important to point out that the vast majority of staff (and people with learning difficulties) were extremely committed, in principle, to the concepts underlying the work. Indeed of all the sites we visited, it was at Edgehill Housing Association that we found the Chief Executive, Head of Personnel and other policy makers to be the most open and enthusiastic about the aims of the work. The Head of Personnel, in particular, was very keen to facilitate ways of involving people with learning difficulties in the recruitment process, even if this meant changing well-established procedures.

Developing knowledge and skills

The pre-training audit provided several opportunities for participants to continue to develop their skills and knowledge about the topic of user involvement in staff recruitment.

Sharing information about the topic by raising awareness of existing good practice within sites

As we discussed in Chapter 4, Bradworth Care Trust had a well-developed policy on involving people with learning difficulties in staff recruitment, copies of which had been sent to all home

managers. Awareness of this document, however, was very low. Of the seven home managers whom we interviewed as part of the pre-training audit, only two referred to it when asked if a policy existed. The others either said that nothing existed, or that they were unsure about the status of the document they had already received:

> "We got a folder last year, but I don't think there is anything in it that says we have to involve people."

Feedback from the pre-training audit raised awareness across the service about the existence of this policy document. Participants were thus able to build on, and develop, the policy throughout the rest of their involvement in the project.

Learning about the benefits, theory and practice of user involvement in recruitment

The pre-training audit at Cherry Tree House showed that staff at both houses were very open to change in the area of user involvement in recruitment. As they spoke to us, they almost appeared to be 'testing out' ideas for doing things differently:

> "Maybe we could change the informal bit? Maybe have an interview with me (the manager) and the residents instead of the chat?"

They were unsure, at this stage, as to whether people with learning difficulties would be interested in, or able, to take part in the recruitment process:

> "It depends on how they progress on the course. We would consider

them being involved in the more formal bit. But to be honest, we've just never thought of it before."

Practitioners at Cherry Tree House acknowledged their own lack of confidence and information about the process of recruiting staff, and expressed a hope that the project would be a learning experience for them, as well as for people with learning difficulties:

"I'm just interested in anything that comes out of it. I do it so rarely that I feel nervous myself."

Keeping commitment going

By the end of each interview, participants had reflected on their site's current practice, evaluated it for themselves, and begun to develop their thinking about how their own individual practice might improve or develop. At this point we supported each participant, or group, to clarify these initial thoughts and to make their goals concrete. The very act of setting goals provided a record of individuals' commitment to user involvement in choosing staff at that point in the project. Each individual participant received a sheet summarising their own specific goals at this stage.

Summary

Chapter 5 has shown how project participants used the pre-training audit as a tool for developing their practice in three key ways:

1. **Evaluating practice** – the process of the pre-training audit itself became a tool for self-reflection and self-awareness
2. **Developing knowledge and skills** – the pre-training audit raised awareness of existing good practice within sites, and of the fact that user involvement in recruitment is possible, particularly among those people with learning difficulties and practitioners who had not yet considered it
3. **Keeping commitment going** – the act of goal setting made commitment concrete and provided a record of the commitment of individuals and sites at this stage of their involvement in the project.

6

Learning and planning

The third step of our work with sites – learning and planning – involved organising and implementing a training programme and encouraging each site to draw up an action plan for the fourth and final step of the project. This chapter charts the ways in which sites developed their practice throughout the learning and planning process.

Training and action planning

The training programme was presented to sites as a model for working together and for involving people with learning difficulties. The underlying premise was that practitioners and people with learning difficulties would be learning together, not just about the recruitment process, but about one another's abilities, needs and perspectives. In this way, we hoped to model good practice in user involvement through the actual format of the training itself.

Our objectives for this stage of the work were to provide opportunities for:

• learning about the benefits, theory and practice of user involvement in the recruitment process and how to

support people with learning difficulties as part of this initiative;
• establishing relationships between groups;
• ensuring shared understanding of concepts;
• reflecting on obstacles and opportunities;
• planning and developing initiatives and identifying key people to take these forward.

We developed a standard training programme based on our existing resource pack (Townsley et al, 1997). (Please see Appendix B for an outline of the training programme.) Each site received a copy of the resource pack and we encouraged participants to continue working through it back in their own home, centre or workplace.

We found that we were able to develop further some of the activities that the pack offered. Drawing up a person specification, in particular, became a strong focus for the training days (Howarth et al, 2000). We also developed additional training and discussion on equal opportunities issues. Although the equal opportunities resources provided by our pack were adequate, we decided to commission a photographer to produce a set of 25 supplementary photographs representing women, men, disabled people, younger people, older people, and people from different ethnic communities. The photo pack also included a set of prints where the same person appeared twice, in two separate photographs, which we hoped would encourage discussion of the influence of different facial expressions, different styles of dress, visibility of an impairment, and so on. These photographs are now available in published form (Gear et al, 2000).

Two members of the project team (Joyce Howarth and Mark Graham) jointly facilitated the training to four separate groups at each site: people with learning difficulties, support staff, managers and policy makers. The basic format for this was that people with learning difficulties and support staff took part in an initial three days' training (Days 1-3), followed by a day for managers and people with learning difficulties together (Day 4), and a further day for policy makers and people with learning difficulties together (Day 5).

Our own learning in relation to the organisation and facilitation of the training days also increased in direct relation to the number of training programmes that we had participated in. Hence, by the time we came to work with Edgehill Housing Association, the format of the training we offered was significantly different from that which we had offered to Attingham City Council. Table 2 (p 29) shows the format of the training programme for each of the five sites.

Cherry Tree House and Danbury House were the smallest of the five sites involved in the project. At each site there was only one person who could be

described as a policy maker, and in reality the roles of manager and policy maker overlapped due to the nature of the service. We thus decided to combine the training for both sites, and to run only Days 1-4.

At Edgehill Housing Association, we ran an extra pre-training day for support staff and managers only. Our work with Edgehill Housing Association had already highlighted some significant resistance to the concept of user involvement and we were keen to tackle this in a direct and positive way. Edgehill Housing Association provided housing services to people with learning difficulties, the majority of whom had high support needs and communication impairments. The pre-training day preceded the main training programme and was an opportunity for support staff and managers across the service to air their views and concerns with the project team. The day was also a chance to provide a more detailed introduction to, and discussion about the topic, of recruitment in general.

We had already identified that our 'standard' training programme was not accessible to the people with learning difficulties living in three particular houses managed by Edgehill Housing Association. We decided, therefore, after discussion with our key contact, that we should offer the opportunity of direct in-house support and discussion with this group of support staff and people with learning difficulties. One of the project team (Mark Graham) spent half a day at each house, discussing the issues, listening to people's concerns, and suggesting ways that staff and people with learning difficulties might work together to recruit new staff. We planned these three half-days to coincide with

Table 2: Training programmes at each site

Training days	Attingham City Council	Bradworth Care Trust	Cherry Tree House and Danbury House	Edgehill Housing Association
Pre-training day	Not applicable	Not applicable	Not applicable	19 support staff and managers
Days 1-3	12 people with learning difficulties; 6 support staff	12 people with learning difficulties; 6 support staff	10 people with learning difficulties; 5 support staff	8 people with learning difficulties; 6 support staff
Day 4	7 people with learning difficulties; 7 managers	8 people with learning difficulties; 11 managers	8 people with learning difficulties; 3 support staff; 3 managers	5 people with learning difficulties; 12 managers
Day 5	6 people with learning difficulties; 8 policy makers	7 people with learning difficulties; 12 policy makers	Not applicable	4 people with learning difficulties; 10 policy makers
Extra days	Not applicable	Not applicable	Not applicable	3 half-days' facilitation/discussion with staff and people with learning difficulties at 3 houses

Days 1-3 of the standard training programme for Edgehill Housing Association. This meant that Mark was absent from the standard training for people with learning difficulties and support staff. Joyce therefore facilitated the training alongside a house manager from Edgehill Housing Association (also an accredited trainer) who stood in for Mark during Days 1-3.

The final part of the training programme was for each site to draw up an action plan and identify who would be responsible for developing the initiative once back on 'home ground'. This was the point at which sites made their own interpretation of the training and development programme offered by the project, and designed their own way forward.

For a more detailed explanation of the format and content of the training see Appendix B and Howarth et al (2000).

Feedback from the training

During the training days the participants produced a large amount of written and illustrated materials. We also took photographs during each of the days and collated these and the other material to produce a series of training notes for each site as a continuing resource for their development work. People with learning difficulties also received a certificate as a record of their involvement.

Following the training, we collected further feedback by asking professionals to complete a training evaluation form. We also sought feedback from people with learning difficulties by conducting group or individual interviews with those people who took part in the training

days. In addition, the project team met to debrief on the training days. These meetings were tape-recorded and transcribed for future reference.

Developing knowledge and skills

The training programme provided an opportunity for the project team to transfer learning about the benefits, theory and practice of involving people with learning difficulties in the recruitment process. In particular, it was a chance for participants to develop a shared understanding of the concepts, increase their knowledge about the recruitment process, and practise their skills in supporting and developing user involvement in recruitment. Feedback on the training demonstrated very clearly that these objectives were achieved for all sites, both for people with learning difficulties and for staff.

Developing a shared understanding of the concepts

If initiatives to promote change are to be successful, they must be underpinned by beliefs and concepts that have been agreed and shared with all the main stakeholder groups. Although this process had already started during the introductory meetings and presentations, the training programme was a prime opportunity for participants to debate and consolidate this, and hopefully to reach a consensus which was acceptable to everyone involved. This objective was achieved during the training, albeit in different ways which reflected each site's initial commitment to the concepts of the project.

Attingham City Council

Participants from Attingham City Council came to the training with a range of viewpoints about how user involvement in recruitment might be implemented in their service. Earlier in this report we saw that the formal agreement of Attingham City Council's involvement in the project was defined by one senior policy maker. This view was different from both the views of other practitioners and people with learning difficulties at that site. It also differed from the model of good practice for user involvement in recruiting set out in Chapter 2.

The first three training days with people with learning difficulties and support workers were very successful. People with learning difficulties had been committed for some time to the concept of user involvement, and the training offered them some practical skills for putting their ideas into practice. Supporters too seemed excited and motivated, and enjoyed learning how to equip people with the skills they would need for future involvement. The fourth day, for people with learning difficulties and managers, also went smoothly. Managers listened to what people with learning difficulties had to say about how they wanted to be involved, and made plans for implementing these ideas in the afternoon session. It appeared that the managers all had a similar vision about how the initiative might work, and a major decision was made to do more pilot work and to go forward with more training for people with learning difficulties.

The fifth day, for policy makers and people with learning difficulties, was more difficult, but no less successful. Many of the policy makers found it hard to work together with people with learning difficulties during the morning session. Communicating in an accessible way was particularly difficult for some people but, to their credit, many people made an effort to overcome their lack of skills, and the trainers reported that by the end of the morning the group was 'positive' although 'not settled'. During the afternoon, when policy makers worked together to find a way forward, the trainers felt that the group seemed more coherent. There was still some disjunction between the views of those for whom the concept of user involvement was still very new, and those for whom it felt long overdue. Thus, some people felt that the group had taken significant steps forwards, while others felt that nothing had changed. Our own view was that, given the starting position of Attingham City Council, a great deal had been achieved in terms of commitment to the concept of real change. Participants had worked hard together to reach agreement about a) the basic concept of user involvement in recruitment as a possibility for their service and b) the specific nature of what this might involve in practice. By the end of the day, participants had drawn up a helpful statement:

> *Clarifying the objectives:*
> We are committed to an empowering recruitment process where users become equal members of the interview panel (apart from the chair). This involves people with learning difficulties in influencing and developing: job descriptions, person specifications, adverts, equal opportunities, shortlisting, information about the service, interviewing, choosing. We will set up a pilot scheme for

recruitment of group workers. We will evaluate it. The intention is to extend it to other staff and other centres.

Bradworth Care Trust

Bradworth Care Trust already appeared to have developed a shared understanding of the concepts, in that a clear organisational policy statement existed. However, the pre-training audit had highlighted the fact that staff awareness of this policy was very patchy, and understanding of its purpose as a learning tool was rarely acknowledged. It appeared that the policy had been 'imposed' without much consultation with staff or people with learning difficulties, and was effectively being ignored by most practitioners. We were impressed with the policy and felt that it reflected a good practice model of user involvement in recruitment. However, it was clear that its existence did not necessarily invoke action.

The role of the training programme seemed to be one of encouraging re-motivation and re-commitment to concepts that were already established in policy. For people with learning difficulties, Days 1-3 were an opportunity to learn, in a relatively formal way, about the recruitment process itself and how they might wish to become involved. The policy advocated involvement at all stages of the recruitment process and training on a house-by-house basis. But the pre-training audit showed that few people with learning difficulties had participated in recruitment, or had taken part in training at their home. Thus the training provided a 'taster' of what the experience might be like, should they wish to get more involved than they were

at present. For support workers, it showed some practical ways to involve people, thereby bringing to life the written policy and training manual.

For managers and policy makers, the training days provided an opportunity to have a long-overdue debate about the benefits, and difficulties, inherent in involving people in recruiting staff. As one person put it:

> "It was a safe environment in which to be frank. A chance to reflect and debate."

By the end of the training programme, practitioners seemed enthused and motivated to get to work on putting the theory into practice. The training had raised awareness of the issues, and of the existence of the policy, and had enabled people to clarify their respective responsibilities. Quite simply, it appeared to have 'got things moving':

> "I now feel we are in a better position to take this work forward. We've accepted the reality and intention of working together to overcome obstacles and we hope to now build on the steps started by the course."

Cherry Tree House and Danbury House

Cherry Tree House and Danbury House had less time to reach a shared understanding, given their training programme was only four days in duration and user involvement in recruitment was a completely new concept for these two sites. The first three days for people with learning difficulties and supporters were an introduction to the idea of the recruitment process and an invitation to get involved. The trainers reported very positive feedback from people with learning difficulties, who clearly enjoyed the opportunity to take part in a training course like this. By Day 4, the people with learning difficulties had become very comfortable with their surroundings and the pace and content of the training. The trainers reported a real sense of 'ownership' by people with learning difficulties, which set the tone for the afternoon session of Day 4. Managers and support workers appeared to accept and share the concept of user involvement at face value – they had seen it in action and now had no reason to doubt that it would work in their service. The only possible problem was that for Danbury House just one practitioner attended the training, on behalf of the wider staff group. Would he be able to enthuse others and enable them to see that user involvement was possible, without the benefit of their seeing it in action for themselves?

Edgehill Housing Association

During our initial meetings with Edgehill Housing Association, we had picked up a certain amount of resistance to the idea of user involvement from support staff. The pre-training day was additional for support staff and managers only, and provided an introduction to the issues, and a chance for them to air their views and concerns. Feedback to the training showed that many people were 'pleasantly surprised' by the experience of attending the training. And in some cases, initial scepticism had been replaced by motivation and enthusiasm:

> "It met my expectations and went further. I had been sceptical. But

> I gained some idea of how we could involve tenants with a profound learning and communication impairment."

During the rest of the training programme, participants demonstrated their commitment to the concept of user involvement that they already shared. They were able to debate the issues, but also to reach a consensus about how to implement the initiative across the service. The sense of this process as positive and substantial is reflected in the following feedback from participants:

> "We debated, but became united."

> "Good group debate. Good consolidation of ideas."

The additional three half-days' work with homes meant that one of the trainers (Mark Graham) was unavailable to co-run Days 1-3 of the standard training programme. We therefore negotiated with Edgehill Housing Association for Joyce Howarth (an accredited trainer) to conduct the first three days alongside one of the service's home managers. This proved to be an immensely effective change to the structure of the work. The home manager was not only an excellent trainer, but also provided a direct link between the training programme and the ongoing development work at the site. She became a champion for the project and was instrumental in supporting ongoing commitment to the shared concepts developed during the training days.

Learning about the recruitment process

The training provided information about the full extent of the recruitment process and enabled both people with learning difficulties, and practitioners, to develop a range of practical skills in the selection and recruitment of staff:

"We did exercises and stuff about choosing people fairly."

"The course looked at the whole process and did not just concentrate on interviewing as other courses have done in the past."

"Since I knew nothing about recruitment, I learnt a lot. Breaking down the process into its different parts really helped."

Several practitioners thought that for people with learning difficulties, taking part in the training had increased not only their learning in this area, but also their general confidence and self-esteem:

"The training has helped people to feel more confident about their abilities and rights."

"It has created interest and confidence for people with learning difficulties."

Developing skills for user involvement in the recruitment process

Practitioner participants told us that the training gave them a range of practical ideas for involving people with learning difficulties in the recruitment process. These ideas covered both training for the recruitment process, and the process itself:

"It gave me a clear understanding of how we could enable our tenants to be fully involved in a meaningful way."

"I now have some ideas that I can put into practice. I feel more confident about supporting the tenants to do more work on this."

For some people, the training increased their awareness of what was possible in this area, particularly if the concept was new to them:

"It made me think about getting people with learning difficulties involved in recruitment, and showed me some ways to do this."

"I suppose I really had not thought about it before. But it showed me a way to involve clients."

Several people said that the training modelled new ways of working with people with learning difficulties, and that in itself this was an immensely powerful tool:

"The methods of training meant that people with learning difficulties and staff learned together in a way that was meaningful for all, learning from each other and about each other's perspectives. The training surpassed my expectations. Learning alongside people with learning difficulties challenged some of my deepest held assumptions about people with learning difficulties. I learned so much more than what I was there for!"

Recognising and valuing one another's abilities, needs and perspectives

Probably the most important outcome of people with learning difficulties and practitioners working together in this way was that the training itself provided strong evidence for involving people with learning difficulties in the recruitment process in an accessible and meaningful way. By working together, people with learning difficulties and practitioners shared their skills and experiences, sometimes to the surprise of some professionals:

> "I was really surprised that people with learning difficulties knew so much about this topic already."

The training enabled sceptics to see for themselves that user involvement is possible and achievable, with training and support:

> "I felt somewhat dubious about this training and what it could achieve, and was pleasantly surprised at the interest shown by people with learning difficulties and the hard work they put into the project."

As one person with learning difficulties summed up:

> "They were surprised we knew so much!"

Working together

In order for the training and development programme to be effective, we knew that the development of good working relationships between and within members of the key stakeholder groups was essential. We had designed the training programme in particular, to model cooperative and collaborative behaviours. Feedback from the five sites indicated that this objective was also achieved successfully.

Establishing and strengthening relationships between groups

Working together allowed participants to develop relationships between and within their stakeholder groups. As practitioners had valued the learning that was an outcome of working together, so too did people with learning difficulties value the process of meeting and working with practitioners on a more equal basis than would normally be the case at their home or day service.

> "The bosses were nice to me. I liked the way they talked to me."

> "Everyone was very polite. They treated us with respect and listened to what we had to say. I'd like to meet some of those people again. It is unusual to be treated like this."

For many policy makers, and some managers, the training also provided a chance to interact with people with learning difficulties and to work together on a concrete task:

> "It was useful to work with people with learning difficulties – we so rarely do!"

> "It was great to see tenants' obvious pleasure and interest and to remind myself of what we are really here for."

Practitioners also appreciated 'time out' to work alongside and share ideas with other professionals, some of whom they had very little direct contact with on a day-to-day basis:

> "It was an opportunity to discuss issues away from units, and to be

creative in devising ways to implement systems for the future."

"It was great to actually work with other managers who otherwise you would only see at meetings."

"It was good to work with people from other houses with a similar tenant group."

Working together on specific tasks was an important way for people to build relationships, and paved the way for developing a shared understanding of the concepts upon which the different initiatives for implementing user involvement in recruitment would be built.

"The support we got on the course was really important. It's too hard to change things on your own."

On a more basic level, participants simply enjoyed meeting each other and working together:

"I didn't expect it to be such good fun! I wish the course went on for longer."

Encouraging practitioners and people with learning difficulties to work together as co-learners

Working together with people with learning difficulties was actually a new experience for some of the participants, and although some people found this hard it was something that they valued nonetheless:

"I was nervous initially, but felt more comfortable as the morning progressed. This was the first time I had worked alongside people with learning difficulties."

Several practitioners were critical of their colleagues' lack of skills in working with people with learning difficulties and suggested that some sort of briefing session before the training would have been helpful:

"Many people in the groups were not skilled in working with people with learning difficulties, so they were not pitching it right – either too complicated or patronising. Needed a short briefing first."

"There was a seeming inability of senior officers to communicate effectively and accessibly with a group of people with learning difficulties with whom they have been working for many years."

Our own view is that these initial difficulties are an intrinsic part of the learning process around user involvement, and that acknowledging them is a precursor to 'letting go' some traditional practices and boundaries. As one person explained:

"It was good to see policy makers and personnel staff slowing down and 'plaining up' their language."

Keeping the perspective of people with learning difficulties at the forefront

The fact that practitioners and people with learning difficulties worked and learned together was a central tenet of the training programme at each site, and was something that was very much valued by both parties. Many practitioners told us that they had learned a lot by simply listening to the ideas and views of people with learning difficulties themselves:

"It gave me a better understanding of the issues from a service user's perspective, which also helped me to clarify my own views and thoughts."

Several other comments reflected the usefulness of working together as a tool for raising awareness among staff of the needs and wishes of people with learning difficulties:

"It gave me an insight into people's thoughts, fears and feelings about unknown people working in their home."

"It gave me time to sit and listen to clients' views about the type of people they wanted."

Practitioners also appreciated the chance to hear direct from people with learning difficulties about how they wanted to be involved in the recruitment process:

"It put the focus very clearly on the needs of people with learning difficulties and highlighted the fact that they have a very strong desire to be part of recruitment."

"The participation of tenants in the training meant that it was not all our assumptions about what tenants think. I enjoyed this and found it honest."

Evaluating practice

Reflection and self-evaluation were important parts of the training programme at each site.

Reflecting on obstacles and opportunities

The project team encouraged participants to identify things that might either inhibit or promote user involvement in recruitment. The purpose of this activity was to encourage sites to focus on the future and to think through how they might manage any difficulties that might emerge.

Time was set aside for this activity at the end of Days 4 and 5 and each site produced a list of obstacles and opportunities that was incorporated into the training notes that they received. Each site also discussed how they would tackle the issues they had identified and this discussion formed the basis of their action plan for taking the initiative forward.

Organising resources

By the end of the learning and planning process, sites were ready to plan and develop their own initiatives for trying out user involvement in recruitment. We encouraged participants to talk about the resource implications of their plans, and to start to make some practical arrangements for taking things forward. The final part of the training programme was for each site to draw up an action plan and identify who would be responsible for developing the initiative once back on 'home ground'. This was the point at which sites made their own interpretation of the training and development programme offered by the project.

By now, they had specified initial goals and identified obstacles and opportunities that might help or hinder their progress.

Next it was time to put their learning into practice and to plan and organise the resources they would need to do this. This included identifying the people, time, support, money, and information needed to make their plans a reality. More details of the different initiatives developed by each site are given in Chapter 7.

Maintaining commitment and changing attitudes

We have already seen how the process of learning and planning together provided strong evidence for participants about the value of involving people with learning difficulties in the recruitment process. Commitment to the concept of user involvement was strengthened by people with learning difficulties and practitioners sharing and developing their skills, knowledge, views and experience.

Promoting the role of people with learning difficulties as central to the success of each initiative

The participation of people with learning difficulties at the planning stage was very important and helped to maintain the sense that their views and perspectives were shaping the planning process. People with learning difficulties drew up their own action plans and presented these to managers and policy makers during the morning sessions on Days 4 and 5. Several practitioners mentioned that during these sessions it really felt as though people with learning difficulties were in control of the initiative, and that they were working together with managers and policy makers in a shared and equal way:

"Tenants took the lead. It was great to see how they could express their opinions in a positive and frank way."

"I felt that we were all working together on shared problems. The barriers that exist between staff and tenants were broken down in a very real sense if only for a few moments at a time but those moments were inestimable in their value to myself."

The value of the first three days' training was clear in this respect. People with learning difficulties were already familiar with the training process, content and format. They felt as though it was 'their' training, and this sense of ownership and commitment came across strongly to managers and policy makers attending Days 4 and 5. Attendance from people with learning difficulties during the morning sessions on Days 4 and 5 was not compulsory. However, we found that the majority of people who had attended the first three days also wished to participate in Days 4 and 5. This was real evidence of a strong commitment to the concept of user involvement, and of wanting to work together with practitioners to achieve change.

The role of 'evidence' in changing attitudes of practitioners

Some participants acknowledged that they had been sceptical about the purpose of the 'Learning to choose staff' project, and its relevance to the clients with whom they worked. They explained, however, that what they had learnt during the training had brought about a change in their attitudes about what might be possible:

Table 3: Participants' perceptions about whether training would help to promote user involvement in recruitment (%)

	Attingham City Council	Bradworth Care Trust	Cherry Tree House and Danbury House	Edgehill Housing Association	Mean totals
Yes	76	95	77	66	78
No	12	0	0	0	3
Don't know	12	5	23	34	19

"I had thought that our client group would not be able to take part in recruitment. But some of the work showed me how people with complex needs can get involved."

As part of the feedback process, we asked participants if they thought that the training programme would help to promote user involvement in recruitment at their site. Table 3 summarises the responses to this question and shows clearly that people felt the training would indeed have an impact on practice in their service.

Clearly, at this point of the project, commitment among participants was running very high. Whether or not this would be maintained in practice was something that we planned to discover during the final stages of the project.

Summary

The training appeared to provide a 'turning point' for the sites. In particular, we noticed that Attingham City Council, Cherry Tree House and Danbury House used the training as an opportunity to reach a consensus about the issues, and to learn to work together in new ways. The planning and learning process enabled people with learning difficulties and practitioners to develop their practice as follows:

- **Developing knowledge and skills** – developing a shared understanding of concepts, learning about the recruitment process, developing skills for user involvement, and recognising and valuing each other's abilities, needs and perspectives
- **Working together** – establishing and strengthening relationships between groups, encouraging practitioners and people with learning difficulties to work together, and keeping the perspective of people with learning difficulties at the forefront
- **Evaluating practice** – reflecting on the obstacles and opportunities to taking user involvement in staff recruitment forward at their sites
- **Organising resources** – as part of the action planning process
- **Maintaining commitment and changing attitudes** – promoting the role of people with learning difficulties as central to success of initiatives, and by using 'evidence' to change attitudes.

7

Developing, supporting and evaluating initiatives

By the end of step 3 – learning and planning – sites were ready to develop their own initiatives for user involvement in recruitment. Chapter 6 showed how the majority of project participants were now committed to taking initiatives forward within their own service. This they did, with some ongoing support from the project team. The fourth and final step of the project was to conduct follow-up and evaluation work at each site. This chapter describes the different site initiatives and explains how the process of evaluating progress continued to enable project participants to develop and change their practice.

Follow-up meetings

We held follow-up meetings with key people at each site two to six months after the training had taken place. The follow-up meetings were a chance to update on progress, to keep the issue alive, and for sites to re-state their goals and action plans. The meetings also provided an opportunity to highlight any interim issues, resource problems, and so on.

At each follow-up meeting we discussed plans and timescales for the final

evaluation and made arrangements for feeding back from the project. Follow-up meetings were not held at Cherry Tree House and Danbury House, due to scheduling problems for the project as a whole. Our telephone contact with Cherry Tree and Danbury had indicated that things were going smoothly and follow-up meetings did not seem necessary. However, in relation to Danbury House, this assumption proved incorrect and a meeting at this stage would indeed have been helpful (as discussed later).

The follow-up meetings, telephone calls and other communication between participants and the project team enabled sites to access ongoing support, advice and information. We tried to respond to requests for additional input where possible. However we knew that our availability was time-limited and that the aim of the project was to empower participants to find their own ways to continue developing and evaluating their practice. In this way, we hoped that key stakeholders at the sites would continue to maintain relationships and to work together without external prompting from us. We also hoped that each site would set up an initiative that would become a focus for continued joint work between people with learning difficulties and practitioners.

Final evaluation

Six months to one year after the training, we interviewed a number of key people at each site from each of the four stakeholder groups. The objectives of the final evaluation were:

- for each site to assess their own progress against the goals they had set themselves;
- for each site to set out their plans for continuing user involvement in recruitment;
- to look for evidence of shifts or changes in practice, policy and attitudes and to assess the progress of each site in relation to our model of good practice for user involvement in recruitment.

The final interviews with practitioners covered the following topic areas:

- **Role of individual staff** – had this changed in any way?
- **Current user involvement in recruitment** – number of new appointments, number of involvement exercises, level of posts, level of involvement at different stages of the recruitment process, any changes to the map of possible involvement identified in the pre-training audit
- **Policy development**
- **Opportunities** – did these still exist? Had they been put to use?
- **Obstacles** – did these still exist? How had they been overcome?
- **Training needs of people with learning difficulties and staff**
- **Experience of taking part in the training** – impact of this on

individuals' practice and perceptions of the role that people with learning difficulties could play in the recruitment process
- **Goal setting and action planning** – what progress had been made? Had goals been achieved?
- **Experience of taking part in the 'Learning to choose staff' project** – Impact on user involvement? Impact on each of the four stakeholder groups?

The interviews with people with learning difficulties at each sites were conducted by members of the Service User Advisory Group (see Appendix A) and covered the following issues:

- **Memories of the training days** – likes, dislikes
- **Impact of the training** – had learning been retained/used?
- **Involvement in staff recruitment since the training**
- **Involvement in decision making**
- **Goal setting and action planning for the future**.

We found that the final evaluation was a helpful way for sites to reaffirm their commitment to the goals they had set themselves. Several sites pointed out that the sheer fact that we were coming back to assess their progress had been a spur to action, thereby emphasising the link between the development and evaluation components of the project. The final interviews were also a chance for several of the key people at each site to meet together once again and revisit their goals, obstacles and opportunities for the initiatives they had established.

Progress of the five sites

The next five sections look at the progress made by participants at each site. Taking each site in turn, we draw out the key issues that promoted change and improved practice, also noting the factors that appeared to impede progress.

Attingham City Council – lost opportunities, lost commitment

Organising resources – planning and developing the initiative

One month after the training, a group of people with learning difficulties and practitioners from Attingham City Council met to follow up the action plan and identify ways forward. This included specifying how each centre would interpret involvement in the recruitment process. These decisions were the outcome of the views and wishes of people with learning difficulties at the centres. The group made some practical suggestions about how to overcome some of the obstacles that had been identified. They also agreed that training should be offered to all people with learning difficulties and that this should be set up as soon as possible. The team leader and a senior support worker agreed to coordinate and evaluate the pilot work. The group agreed to meet again to discuss how the different models of involvement had progressed. It was also proposed that a group of senior staff would meet separately, to work on the policy level of the initiative.

A further follow-up meeting with the project team, was held five months after the training programme. The team leader, senior support worker and two policy makers attended this session, and plans for the initiative were discussed further and in some detail. Agreed action included:

- to plan and implement training for all people with learning difficulties;
- to establish a service-wide panel of people with learning difficulties who would act as 'roving recruiters';
- to evaluate the work and make necessary changes to policy.

We conducted the final evaluation 13 months after the follow-up meeting with Attingham City Council. At that time, it appeared that no further action or progress had been made in relation to the planned initiative. Recruitment practice at the centres had continued in the same way as it had before the site participated in the project – people with learning difficulties were still involved in the interview process on a centre-by-centre basis. On the positive side, one of the two centres that had taken part in the project had made efforts to improve the way in which people with learning difficulties were involved in recruitment. This centre had involved an independent advocate who provided support and opportunities for practice to the people with learning difficulties who took part in the formal interview. However, we discovered that several subsequent opportunities for involvement at this centre were 'lost', since an independent advocate was not available to support people with learning difficulties. So what had happened to forestall such promising progress?

Organising resources – difficulties in responding to challenges as they arose

From our interviews with people with learning difficulties and practitioners, it appeared that there were a number of reasons for the loss of momentum with

Attingham City Council. The first problem occurred when the senior support worker who had taken joint responsibility (with the team leader) for developing the initiative went on extended sick leave. Her role was not delegated to another person, which meant that full responsibility for progress was in the hands of the team leader.

At that time, Attingham City Council was undergoing a great deal of organisational change. A review of day services had recently been conducted, and the outcomes resulted in huge changes to service delivery. Given this situation it was inevitable that less priority would be given to the site's initiative on user involvement in staff recruitment, simply as a result of competing priorities and demands.

Working together – difficulties in maintaining relationships between stakeholder groups

Another issue that emerged was that there appeared to be a stalemate over whether it was the responsibility of day centre managers, or policy makers, to initiate action. Support staff and managers told us that they were waiting for a change in policy before they could make changes at operational level:

> "As officers of (Attingham City Council), we have to do recruitment in a certain way, however inflexible this may seem to people with learning difficulties. We can't change our official practice without a change from the Personnel Department."

Indeed, our interview with the centre managers highlighted their concern that more progress had not been made at the policy level, and produced a list of

questions for policy makers that they wished the project team to ask on their behalf.

The policy makers, for their part, explained that they were committed to change but had been awaiting the requests of staff, people with learning difficulties and managers. As the training and staff development manager put it:

> "I am ready to go ahead and book the trainers. The budget is there to pay them. I've been waiting for names to come from the centres about who wants to take part."

Developing skills and knowledge – lack of opportunities for putting learning into practice

The lack of training had an impact on people with learning difficulties. Without it, people had not had the chance to practise their recruitment skills, or to maintain their enthusiasm for the initiative as a whole. Both people with learning difficulties and practitioners referred to their involvement in the project as a 'lost opportunity'. Indeed, several people commented that such a loss of impetus was not uncommon throughout the service:

> "We are very good at starting things, but not at finishing them. Things get lost in mid-air, especially when other things get in the way."

Evaluating the process – reflecting on current practice and obstacles and revising plans for the initiative

During the final interview with three of the policy makers, they admitted that the service manager should take responsibility for clarifying the situation for everyone. The decision was whether to continue with the initiative now, and if so how, or whether to put the initiative on hold until a later date when staff would be less busy than at present.

"We can encourage practice, but without operational management we cannot push it. So obviously it has got to be more directive. Unless it comes from the top, it's not going to happen. That must be an overview of the very disappointing outcome. And we need to decide now how to move it on, or be clear about it not moving. Then at least everyone knows clearly where we are, and what is permissible for the centres to do in the interim."

The interview with policy makers showed the important role that the evaluation process played in development work with the sites. The three policy makers who took part in the interview – personnel manager, training and staff development manager and the service manager – had not met as a group to discuss the initiative since the 'Learning to choose staff' training programme. The questions we posed enabled them to reflect on the 'disappointing outcome', and to try to find an interim solution. As the interview came to a close, the three policy makers agreed to pursue an immediate funding opportunity in order to buy-in a project worker who might reinstate the initiative.

Summary of Attingham City Council's progress

Attingham City Council's plans were designed to build on and improve existing practice in user involvement in recruitment. Initial progress at this site was very promising. Immediately following the training programme, it

appeared that a great deal of progress had been made, particularly in terms of reaching agreement about shared objectives and in building relationships between groups. However, in the longer term, relationships between groups were not maintained, and participants were not able to respond to challenges such as the loss of active champions, the impact of wider organisational change, and a lack of opportunities for practice. These obstacles depleted the reserves of commitment generated during earlier stages of the project, and were responsible for stopping Attingham City Council's embryonic initiative in its tracks.

Bradworth Care Trust – loss of a champion, loss of commitment, emergence of a new champion?

Organising resources – planning and developing the initiative

We conducted a follow-up meeting with Bradworth Care Trust three months after the training programme. Things were going well. The service development manager had taken responsibility for keeping the action plan on track, and had set up a meeting with other practitioners to discuss the format and content of the proposed training programme. He also asked for written feedback on Bradworth Care Trust's involvement in the project, which we prepared and sent to him.

We did not attend the second progress meeting. However, our key contact sent us copies of the document that was the result of the discussion, entitled 'Consultation paper on the involvement of people with learning difficulties in the recruitment and selection of staff'. In addition, a separate strategy document on 'User involvement for people with learning disabilities living in (Bradworth

Care Trust's) homes' had been produced, also by the service development manager (our key contact), which set the initiative in the wider context of user involvement across the organisation. This document set out the organisation's financial commitment to user involvement:

"Because user involvement is an organisational priority, the trustees have agreed to put by an extra sum of £30,000 to the Training and Development Budget for the year 1999-2000 to help get these initiatives off the ground."

The service development manager sent out the consultation paper for comment. Ten months after Bradworth Care Trust had taken part in the training programme, plans for a 'Pilot project on the involvement of people with learning difficulties in the recruitment and selection of staff' were finalised and circulated. This document clarified the site's plans to:

- ensure that people with learning difficulties living in Bradworth Care Trust's homes were involved in the staff recruitment and selection process;
- ensure the process balanced good practice and financial constraints;
- ensure both users and homes staff were aware of employment law and policies;
- establish a rolling programme of training over two to three years with homes staff and people with learning difficulties being supported to take over the role of facilitators from external trainers.

The plans for the pilot work were realistic, achievable and in keeping with our model of good practice. Moreover, they also extended the scope of the initiative to include people with learning difficulties as trainers. At this point, largely as a result of the efforts of the service development manager, it seemed that the 'Learning to choose staff' project had had a significant impact on practice and policy at Bradworth Care Trust.

Commitment and attitudes – uncertainty over the extent and nature of commitment to the concepts

One month after the plans for the pilot project had been finalised and circulated, the service development manager left Bradworth Care Trust for a new job. To his credit, all the necessary groundwork had been done, in preparation for the ongoing initiative. We visited the service to conduct the final evaluation 13 months after the training programme had finished, and two months after the departure of our key contact. We interviewed the personnel manager and head of learning disabilities services, who explained that the post of service development manager no longer existed. Instead, the duties that had previously been carried out by our key contact person had been 'shared out' among various practitioners. The head of service now had policy responsibility for user involvement. She admitted that there had been 'some slippage' in terms of the organisation's progress, but assured us that commitment towards the initiative was still there. She appeared a little unsure as to the status of the existing documents, and to the status of the initiative as a whole:

"Where do they [the documents] fit in? Where does this scheme fit in with the wider implications of an operational strategy? I would suggest that although it says 'policy' it is more of a statement of principle. And although it states that 'people with learning difficulties will be involved', and that is what we aim for, that is part of our mission which is being reviewed since we last met, so it's not all people with learning difficulties and it's not all homes. We haven't come that far down the road."

Organising resources – responding to new challenges

The head of service and the personnel manager also introduced a new concern – the need for a speedy recruitment process:

"There is also the issue about how do we get the balance of efficient and speedy recruitment and compromise that in line with user involvement ... it does slow down the whole process, and quite often we will lose interested people, so that's one of the risks."

This was not an issue that had been highlighted previously, and indeed was likely to be incompatible with effective user involvement. As Bradworth Care Trust's own strategy document stated, "the time involved in carrying through [user involvement] initiatives cannot be underestimated".

Commitment – the impact of losing a champion

Responsibility for continuing Bradworth Care Trust's initiative on user involvement in recruitment had fallen to one home manager. He was keen to see progress, but questioned the ongoing commitment of the organisation as a whole. He explained that since the departure of the service development manager, user

involvement across the service was no longer seen as a priority:

"Service user involvement has gone to nil. There is absolutely none whatsoever. It's such a shame. So users are losing out and there has been no consultation with users or their managers. This is what has happened and that is the barrier and that is why I am really loathe to do this unless there is a commitment to user involvement."

He felt that the continued involvement of external facilitators would be extremely helpful to the progress of the initiative, particularly in terms of re-establishing lost enthusiasm and commitment:

"I think it needs someone like Joyce or Mark to come back for a day and do some more action planning with us. Because they were inspirational and they had no boundaries. You can get bogged down in the day-to-day."

Maintaining commitment – the role of evidence

The home manager also felt that staff attitudes were still a barrier. Yet he felt it might be possible to overcome this difficulty if sufficient examples of successful involvement were presented to the 'doubters':

"Those teams need to see it working. They say 'it works with some homes but not with others'. Not true! The home I represent has residents who don't use words at all, but they have been involved in choosing their staff. But I'm not saying that I am the best person to train other people. I can show them what we have done, and be really positive and enthusiastic about it, but I can't be as inspirational as Joyce and Mark were."

Summary of Bradworth Care Trust progress

For Bradworth Care Trust, a great deal of excellent planning and policy work had been undertaken during the earlier stages of the project. However, these plans had not yet been put into practice and the departure of the service development manager left Bradworth Care Trust without an active champion at policy-making level. The continued existence of the initiative was precarious and subject to a number of new barriers that had the potential to undermine the excellent progress already made. There appeared to be significant uncertainty and some resistance among policy makers in relation to the extent and nature of commitment to the concept of user involvement in recruitment. Although a new champion appeared to be waiting in the wings, it was not clear whether he would be able to overcome the numerous barriers and sustain the initiative in the longer term. As a home manager, the new champion had no policy making responsibility and appeared to be waging a lone campaign in the face of resistance from staff at other levels.

Cherry Tree House – learning together, building commitment

Organising resources and building commitment – planning, developing and documenting the initiative

We carried out the final evaluation at Cherry Tree House seven months after the training had taken place. The progress made by participants at Cherry Tree House surpassed our expectations. Since the training, people with learning difficulties and practitioners at Cherry Tree House had produced the following documents:

- An organisational policy on 'Choosing staff', which clarified the overall commitment to the concept, and specified that each unit was responsible for writing its own procedures to meet the needs and interests of those particular residents. The policy also stated that each unit was required to produce an information pack which could be used as a communication tool by people who communicated non-verbally and who wished to take part in the recruitment process.
- Written procedures on 'Residents' involvement in selection' for each unit, or house. These set out, in some detail, the processes whereby people with learning difficulties at each unit would take part in recruitment. People with learning difficulties themselves had been fully involved in the production of these procedures and their chosen forms of participation were included.
- Lists of questions to be asked by residents, again for each unit or house. These incorporated the exact wording suggested by residents. Several lists also included symbols and pictures.
- Scoring grids, which allowed a score to be given for each question asked.
- A sheet for written feedback from each recruitment process, including a record of answers given by candidates to residents' questions.

In addition, staff from one of the houses that had taken part in the project had updated their general recruitment procedure, which included re-writing the list of questions and the mechanism for assessment in order to dovetail this with the scoring grid drawn up by the residents.

Developing skills and knowledge – putting learning into practice

Since the training, residents from both houses had taken part in a recruitment exercise, which had provided an excellent opportunity for putting their newly developed skills into practice. Both houses had developed similar procedures. Residents were involved in sending out application forms to prospective candidates. When a short-list had been drawn up by the manager, candidates were invited to attend two interviews: one with the people with learning difficulties, and one with the manager. The residents then conducted their interview, which involved discussing the information pack with candidates, asking questions, scoring candidates, and feeding back the scores to the manager. Following the second interview, both sets of scores were added to one scoring grid and a decision was made based on the combined scores from both interviews. A resident then telephoned the successful candidate to inform them of the outcome. Confirmation was also followed up in writing.

Organising resources – responding to challenges

In both houses, a combination of factors had meant that only one candidate actually turned up on the interview day. And in one house, the candidate withdrew from the application process before the second interview, which meant that residents did not get the chance to complete the full recruitment process. Nevertheless, the procedures were in

place for future recruitment exercises, and residents had had one opportunity to conduct the majority of the process in a 'real' environment.

Working together – keeping the initiative alive

Practitioners at Cherry Tree House explained that establishing user involvement in recruitment as an agenda item at the cross-organisational strategy planning meetings had been instrumental in bringing about the significant changes that had occurred.

> "After the training it felt like things had gone a bit slack. Then the issue of user involvement was raised at our strategy meetings, and it was kept on the agenda to make sure that people followed up some of the action points from it. It was the people that had gone on the training that really kept it moving and kept checking up that others had done what they were supposed to have done."

Developing skills and knowledge – sharing information about the topic

The practitioners who had taken part in the project explained that, at first, other staff within the service were unsure, as they themselves had been initially, that residents could be meaningfully involved in recruitment. To counter this, the participants had spent some time talking through the outcomes of the training, referring to the training notes in order to 'prove' that learning had occurred. Even though the proprietor had attended half a day's training, she had not been convinced by our arguments that user involvement was a 'good thing'. However, once she had seen for herself the nature and extent of the work achieved by staff and people with learning difficulties, it appeared that her attitude changed dramatically:

> "I think to start off with (the proprietor) was not very positive at all. But I think that as we moved on she became more positive. She certainly listened to what we had done and has taken it on board. And I think she now views it as being very useful. It does need her approval and input to go ahead, and she has been quite pushy in insisting that every unit made their contribution and got on with it."

Commitment – the role of evidence

There was a sense from those we interviewed that this initiative was only accepted, by themselves and others, once proof of its real feasibility had been presented to them. For the project participants this evidence was provided by the training, and in terms of the subsequent enthusiasm and skills of the people with learning difficulties:

> "At the beginning, I must admit that I thought it would be something that they wouldn't get much out of, or be particularly interested in. But it has really surprised me how much interest they have shown in it, and when they actually interviewed someone recently, they were so professional and it was really wonderful to see it. It has taught me not to underestimate them."

For others who had not taken part in the project, it was the evidence of work completed, and successful recruitment exercises undertaken, that brought about a shift of opinion. The role of project participants as 'champions' was also important. They had found time to continue work on the initiative and had kept the views and needs of people with learning difficulties at the forefront when developing their new procedures. The enthusiasm of these staff was palpable, and had clearly 'rubbed off' on their colleagues.

Summary of Cherry Tree House progress

It appeared that participants' involvement in the project had made a significant, long-term impact on both policy and practice at Cherry Tree House. Reasons for this included a well-planned and documented initiative including written statements of organisation commitment to the concepts, opportunities for putting learning into practice, responding to challenges, keeping the initiative alive, sharing information about the topic and using evidence to build commitment. The clear enthusiasm and skills of people with learning difficulties were also a key issue in promoting change at Cherry Tree House.

We were amazed, and delighted, at such far-reaching outcomes. And as one practitioner summed up:

> "Had I not gone on the course I would still be struggling. It was not something that would have occurred to anyone had you not come along and suggested it. We needed that chunk of training to get us going."

Danbury House – lack of support and opportunities, loss of commitment

Developing skills and knowledge – lack of opportunities for putting learning into practice

We visited Danbury House, as part of the final evaluation, nine months after the training programme. There had been no new appointments made over that period; hence there had been no opportunities for involvement by people with learning difficulties in the recruitment process. This was an obstacle that it was not possible to overcome.

The support worker had organised some refresher training as planned, but this had happened immediately after the training programme and had not been followed up by any additional work or practice of skills learnt:

> "The residents that had been on the course spoke to all of the other residents about what they had done, because they were so enthusiastic about it. Then we did some refresher training days very soon afterwards, because people were still interested in carrying on learning a bit more. But then when it became clear that we wouldn't need to be advertising and interviewing new staff for a while, I think everyone just lost interest.... But I think that when the opportunity arises to get involved in it again then their motivation will come back."

Organising resources – new challenges

> Although it had been one of their key goals, the residents had yet to produce an information pack for their home. The manager explained that residents had

been very busy with other activities since the training days and that they had not had a sufficiently long period of time in which to put an information pack together. He also pointed out that the majority of residents were engaged in activities during the day, which was the time when interviews would be carried out:

> "It is actually quite difficult because the majority of the residents are now out in the day time and my interviewing time has to be in the day, it is really, really difficult to try and coordinate all of this."

For this reason, he proposed that the plan to involve people with learning difficulties in an additional interview might not be possible.

> "What I hope to do is to get them to identify a list of important questions that they feel are key points for the staff that they want in their home. Then I will ask that person the questions, because the problem is that not all of the residents are here through the day."

Commitment and attitudes – responding to different levels of commitment and challenging attitudes

During the group interview we conducted with the manager and the support worker, it became clear that there was some disjunction between their perceptions of the abilities of people with learning difficulties as recruiters. The manager had a 'pre-training' view of some of the problems that people might experience, as evidenced by the following comments:

"I think that a lot of residents will judge someone on how they look."

"The residents might think, 'Oh we can't be bothered'."

"Looking at it realistically with the residents that we have, which one of the residents do you think would be able to do an interview, in a professional manner?"

The support worker challenged the last of these comments, suggesting that she felt having residents involved in the interview itself would indeed give a very good impression to prospective employees:

"Well they have done the training and you know the interviews that we did were quite realistic. So I think that as long as they have plenty of practice, and we involve the people that really understand what the interview process is all about, then I think it would work fine."

Following a lengthy discussion, the manager finally capitulated:

"Well actually at the end of the day it's not my decision, it's up to all the people who live here, so it's not worth us sitting here and having a long conversation about it, the best way is to have a go and see what happens. If it works, then it will become policy that people are involved. If it doesn't work then we can add it as an amendment to say instead that residents can be involved at x, y, z stage, or whatever."

This was a very positive outcome, and showed how the evaluation process itself was able to feed directly into development work with sites. However, it also indicated that an earlier meeting (such as the omitted follow-up meeting) might have had a much greater impact on practice at Danbury House than we had imagined.

Commitment and attitudes – difficulties with defining the extent and nature of commitment and the role of evidence

As a 'lone voice', the support worker probably needed more external support than we were able to offer. She was left with the responsibility not only of progressing the initiative itself, but also of trying to convince other staff and the manager that user involvement was a good idea. Commitment to the concepts had clearly not been agreed within the service to the extent that we had initially believed. The role that the training played in convincing dissenters was key here; it was also clear that the manager's absence from the training days left him with an outdated perception about the abilities of the residents as recruiters. Had he participated, perhaps the impact of the project on practice at Danbury House might have been very different.

Summary of Danbury House progress

For Danbury House, it appeared that the project did help to bring about change as a direct result of people's participation in the training, but that this was not sustained in the longer term. Reasons for this included lack of opportunities for putting learning into practice, difficulties in responding to new challenges, and uncertainty over commitment to the concepts. The champion at Danbury House was a lone voice, and was not working at a management, or policy making level. Despite her clear ability to challenge attitudes and use evidence to promote the concept of user involvement in recruitment, without managerial or organisational support, it seemed unlikely that the initiative would flourish.

Edgehill Housing Association – working together to maintain commitment at all levels

Organising resources and evaluating the process – planning and developing the initiative and reflecting on current practice

We had a follow-up meeting with Edgehill Housing Association's service development manager one month after the training, to follow up on the progress of the action plan. He had taken responsibility for moving forward with the initiative at the organisational and strategic levels. Meanwhile the co-trainer/ home manager and a support worker (who had also taken part in the training) were responsible for operational outcomes and were setting up ongoing work and training with people with learning difficulties.

One month later the service development manager met with other policy makers, including the head of personnel. At that meeting the action plan was reviewed, and names and dates added to specify who was responsible for what tasks and by when. It is worth listing the new set of actions since they show a continued and sustained commitment to the initiative by the Housing Association:

- update lead regional manager for service user participation of the actions that we have agreed;
- review recruitment and selection procedure to include commitment to service user participation;
- review job descriptions and person specification for support workers to take account of views forwarded by people with learning difficulties involved in the research project;
- review involvement of people with learning difficulties in review of probationary periods;
- review involvement of people with learning difficulties in induction process;
- review joint training for people with learning difficulties and staff – for example, assertiveness, health and safety;
- draw up a practice statement regarding service user participation in range of ways;
- extend the work to other areas across the organisation; home manager and support worker responsible for this to attend area managers' meeting;
- ensure commitment to service user participation is reflected in Operations Workplan as well as Regional Plans;
- prepare article for key publication (for example, Community Care) about the work that has been completed to date;
- prepare 'flyer' suitable for enclosure with tenders and marketing material regarding the work that has been completed to date;
- approach appropriate agencies to see if we can secure grants for new developmental work;
- identify one of the Board members as a champion of service user participation;
- research possibility of six-month secondment post to take this work forward.

Developing skills and knowledge – continuing to share information about the topic and to learn about the benefits, theory and practice of user involvement in recruitment

We conducted an additional follow-up meeting (one month after the training) with the home manager who had acted as co-trainer alongside Joyce Howarth. She explained that a 'choosing staff' group for people with learning difficulties had been set up, which she facilitated. She highlighted the fact that she had both enjoyed the training, and increased her knowledge and skills in the process:

"I thoroughly enjoyed it. Having co-trained alongside Joyce, I now feel that I can continue that, cascade it, take it forward. And I've learnt for myself about the recruitment process, how to support user involvement in recruitment and about the skills needed to do training on recruitment."

She also reiterated the amount that seemed to have been learnt by the people with learning difficulties who attended:

"It is such a joy to see people get down to it. I really feel it can help them to pick out those professionals who just give the 'spiel' in an interview."

Commitment – responding to different levels of commitment and challenging attitudes where necessary

The home manager pointed out that as someone who was herself working directly with people with learning difficulties, it was more likely that she could have an impact on dissenting and doubting staff than, say, a policy maker could:

"As a manager I'm 'one of the staff'. I can put them right on it. I know that people with learning difficulties can do it and that it works."

Developing skills and knowledge – sharing information, keeping learning up-to-date and providing opportunities for practise

We carried out the final evaluation six months after Edgehill Housing Association's participation in the training programme. Over this period it seemed that progress at all levels had been substantial and sustained. The 'choosing staff' group for people with learning difficulties had met twice and three more meetings were planned. In their first meeting the group had reviewed the work they had done on the training, planned the format and content of the forthcoming meetings and set up ground rules. At the second meeting, people with learning difficulties had worked on producing information packs for their homes. At subsequent meetings, the group planned to observe some up-coming interviews for new staff; practise their listening skills and conduct a mock interview; and develop a list of interview questions. Their goal was to take part in interviews for generic relief workers at some point after the fifth meeting, as a way of practising their skills and keeping their interest in the concept current. In the meantime, if vacancies came up in their own homes, they intended to get involved in the whole recruitment process. The suggestion to observe the interviews for bank staff came from one particular service user who had heard, from staff at his home, that these were going ahead.

The group had applied to the head office of the organisation for a small sum of money to fund their training and development work, which they were granted. They planned to use some of this money to buy films for an instant camera. They would then be able to photograph candidates in order to help them remember who said what in an interview situation.

Working together – identifying key people while keeping the perspective of people with learning difficulties at the forefront

Practitioners at Edgehill Housing Association told us that plans were afoot to extend the training and development work with people with learning difficulties to other areas. In fact, in one area, this was already in progress, and was the result of one policy maker's enthusiasm to get things moving following her involvement in the training programme:

> "He (area manager) has actually altered the approach considerably. He came down to the policy makers' day and within a month she had put together a whole strategy plan, and they are now doing their recruitment in a totally different way. There is a lot of reprovision going on, where people are either moving out of home, or out of another service. And (the area manager) is having meetings with the new tenants and asking them what they expect, what they want to look for, what is important to them (about new staff)."

When we visited, policy development on user involvement in recruitment for the organisation as a whole was in progress.

Practitioners stressed the importance of developing policy that reflected the good practice and lessons that were being learnt from the work of the service user group:

> "I think what needs to be written is that there needs to be clear guidance around the training and practice for people with learning difficulties – how it should happen. And that doesn't mean just sticking a token person on the panel. We need to learn how to get it nearly right prior to the policy being written. If the policy reflects our experience then it will be a much more meaningful policy."

Evaluating the process – reflecting on current practice and revising plans if necessary

Practitioners at Edgehill Housing Association were keen to review not only the progress of the initiative, but also their employment and recruitment procedures more generally to ensure a coordinated approach. The head of personnel also explained his wish to make recruitment procedures more accessible to everyone:

> "We have been trying to make our policies clearer for everyone, because I think a lot of staff say they are too lengthy, too wordy, and I agree they could be a lot plainer. When we do the review we are going to take into consideration how we can make more of a commitment to service user involvement. Rather than having it just as a statement it will probably need some sort of appendix which says this is how it can happen."

Commitment and attitudes – using evidence of success to promote and maintain commitment

The issue of commitment at an operational level was also raised by practitioners. Once again, people stressed the importance of showing that user involvement can work, and providing examples and evidence for this. The commitment from senior policy makers appeared to have been strengthened by their involvement in the training programme:

> "We walked into a very ordered, in control situation, where we were there as equal partners with the tenants and you get into a position where all those doubts start to melt away. I say now that I have never seen the chief executive and the chair of board so enthusiastic about anything, they still talk about it regularly."

Working together – identifying key people, supporting champions and developing relationships while keeping the views of people with learning difficulties at the forefront

The site was planning to share information and enthusiasm about the initiative across its UK areas in several ways. The home manager who facilitated the 'choosing staff' group hoped to run a workshop at the organisation's annual conference. The service development manager hoped to identify champions in each geographical area who could take the initiative forward in different ways, from the perspective of the people with learning difficulties with whom they worked. These champions would then form a working party, or network, which could keep tabs on progress across the organisation as a whole. Their starting point, however, would be to meet the

'choosing staff' group and learn from their experiences so far:

> "If we get a rep, a champion or two from each area down to meet the group and see the work they have done, then that is a really good way of getting them to see evidence, to be enthused all over again, and maybe acknowledging that it is a long process."

The local champions could then 'spread the word' among people with learning difficulties and practitioners, who hopefully, by getting involved in the process and training, would see that user involvement in recruitment was possible and achievable:

> "It's a matter of getting people on board, and if we can get one or two people in an area then it's amazing how it can change. I think a lot will be overcome by actually being involved in the process and thinking 'well, it did work', and this is really where I think the training days worked, because it proved it could be done."

Evaluating the process – reviewing and documenting ongoing work, sharing this with others, and revising plans if necessary

The service development manager had produced a written report about the site's work on the project, which he planned to disseminate across the organisation. This document acted as a written declaration of Edgehill Housing Association's commitment to continued user involvement, and highlighted the impact of their involvement in the 'Learning to choose staff' project.

"Tenants and staff at all levels have indicated very strongly how valuable and enjoyable they found the experience of participating in this project. What remains now is to maintain the momentum and to ensure that this experience becomes part of the fabric of our service."

There also appeared to be a possibility of employing, or seconding, a project worker who could coordinate and develop the initiative:

"We have also looked at going to senior management for a six month secondment post to take it forward, because the more we went through it, the more we realised how much work is involved."

Practitioners were still aware that commitment from a certain section of support staff was lacking. They were keen to ensure that, as the initiative developed, this group of staff and the people they supported were not forgotten:

"I have a disappointment around that and I think 'could I have done more?' Is there any way we could have done it better, or differently? It's almost like we were preaching to the converted. If we had got people whose attitudes weren't quite where we would like them to be, then it would have been an ideal situation. But I don't think those staff made that leap. I think that what they did on their training day [pre-training day] was a step, but now they have been able to leave it alone because it doesn't affect them."

The quotation above is clear evidence of Edgehill Housing Association's continued commitment to user involvement in recruitment. They had made a great deal of progress over the lifetime of the project, but they were not complacent about the work that was still to be done. People with learning difficulties had yet to be involved in the actual process of recruiting staff, although it was clear that the stages of commitment and planning had been fully achieved. As the service development manager summed up:

"It's had an impact, we have yet to see the fruits of it. It is great that we were knocked for six, it's great that we are committed and have been all along. We want some substance behind it now, we want some action."

Summary of Edgehill Housing Association progress

By the end of the project, it seemed that Edgehill Housing Association had made significant changes to its practice and policy. More importantly it appeared that the way in which these changes had been implemented would enable the initiative to be sustained in the longer term. At Edgehill Housing Association, policy was informed and led by practice, and the views and experiences of people with learning difficulties were kept at the forefront of the developing initiative. Practitioners and people with learning difficulties continued to work together and share skills and knowledge. There were opportunities for keeping learning up-to-date and for putting this learning into practice. Several key people at both policy and practice level acted as champions for the initiative and continued to identify other key people to take the work forward. All new work promoted the centrality of the role of people with learning difficulties and kept their views at the forefront of developments. Practitioners were able to successfully respond to challenges and different levels of commitment from others and to use evidence to promote and maintain commitment among staff and people with learning difficulties. Finally, practitioners and people with learning difficulties at Edgehill Housing Association evaluated and documented their progress, shared this with others and were willing to develop new plans in order to respond to any challenges that arose.

Summary

Table 4 summarises the outcomes of the 'Learning to choose staff' project for sites, in terms of the progress they had made by the date of the final evaluation.

This chapter has shown how generating and maintaining *commitment* is a fundamental foundation for developing initiatives to promote change and improve practice. When commitment is lost, challenged or eroded, even the most well-planned initiatives will flounder.

The five sites that took part in the 'Learning to choose staff' project encountered the following *threats to generating and maintaining commitment* to the initiatives they set up:

- competing priorities, such as wider organisational change;
- lack of, or loss of, an active champion;
- lack of opportunities for putting learning into practice;
- difficulties in maintaining relationships between groups;
- uncertainty, or confusion, over the extent and nature of commitment to the initiative;
- no champions at policy level;
- resistance and lack of enthusiasm.

For Attingham City Council, Bradworth Care Trust and Danbury House, these threats appeared difficult, if not impossible, to overcome.

Table 4: Summary of the impact of the project on policy and practice at the five sites

	Changes made to policy?	Changes made to practice?	Have people with learning difficulties recruited any staff yet?
Attingham City Council	No	No	Yes
Bradworth Care Trust	Yes	No	No
Cherry Tree House	Yes	Yes	Yes
Danbury House	No	No	No
Edgehill Housing Association	Yes	Yes	No

For Cherry Tree House and Edgehill Housing Association, however, practitioners and people with learning difficulties seemed able to overcome these threats by taking advantage of the following *opportunities for developing and maintaining commitment*:

- the existence of active champions at policy and practice levels;
- identifying key people and developing new champions for the initiative;
- maintaining relationships between groups;
- responding to organisational and attitudinal challenges;
- using evidence of success as a tool to encourage and enthuse others;
- keeping the initiative alive;
- sharing information about the topic with others;
- keeping the views of people with for learning difficulties at the forefront so that policy was led and informed by practice;
- documenting and reviewing practice and obstacles;
- revising plans, and wider practice, where necessary.

Access to ongoing support and advice from a project team who had dedicated time for working with sites was also important for developing and maintaining commitment. Participants valued the team as external facilitators who had 'no boundaries' and could encourage and enthuse others to see the importance of people with learning difficulties as recruiters. The evaluation component of the project also played a useful role in enabling participants to reflect and assess the work they were developing.

8

Strategies for promoting change and improving practice

This report has described the work of a project that aimed to promote the involvement of people with learning difficulties in staff recruitment. We achieved this aim by designing a training and development programme that, we hoped, would stimulate changes to practice. We evaluated this process by collecting data in order to describe what happened when professionals and people with learning difficulties were actively encouraged to put ideas from research into practice. This chapter concludes with a summary of strategies for promoting change and improving practice, with reference to the evidence-base provided by the work of the 'Learning to choose staff' project.

Evaluating the process of the 'Learning to choose staff' project

Our previous research (Townsley and Macadam, 1996; Townsley et al, 1997) had already highlighted key evidence about what works in implementing user involvement in recruitment. Using this evidence, we developed a set of good practice recommendations that informed the content and structure of the 'Learning to choose staff' project. Our programme

of work with each of the five sites followed a four-step format:

1. Bringing people together
2. Reflecting on current practice
3. Learning and planning
4. Developing, supporting and evaluating initiatives.

At each of the four steps, we disseminated key findings about the value of involving people with learning difficulties in recruitment. We also provided opportunities for participants to practise skills, learn and work together, and evaluate their own practice and progress. The participation of people with learning difficulties at each step, and the co-learning model adopted during the training programme (step 3), allowed us to model good practice in user involvement throughout the project.

Reflecting on obstacles to the project

The time constraints of the project and the need to keep the work within budget allowed little room for making significant changes to the structure of the project, or for responding to issues or problems that arose. The pace and very defined structure meant that some stages had to be omitted in order to keep the work on schedule. Another issue was our reliance on the goodwill of the key contacts – when this failed, or became problematic, the smooth running of the project was affected on many levels.

Reflecting on successful aspects of the project

Opportunities, or things that were successful, included regular progress meetings, written minutes of all meetings with sites and with the project team and maintaining log-books or notes of conversations with participants and decisions agreed. We also found that providing sites with 'branded' project information was very helpful as it encouraged a sense of belonging to the project as a whole. Summarising interviews and goals for participants was also a useful way of promoting the idea of a shared project, with shared goals.

While including five sites generated a great deal of work, it also meant that a wide range of people, needs, interests, attitudes and services were represented. Despite the time constraints, we were able to respond to the individual needs of each site, and in particular to the challenges highlighted by Edgehill Housing Association. Maintaining a degree of flexibility and being pragmatic about what it was possible to achieve within the limits of the project was an effective approach to doing development work of this sort. We realised that it was not always essential to adhere slavishly to the structure of the project in order to achieve the objectives of the work.

We also recognised, in retrospect, the importance of spending adequate time on the initial stages of the work with sites.

The introductory meetings and presentations played more of a role in the development side of the work than we had envisaged. Similarly, the link between evaluation and ongoing development was highlighted by the pre-training audit, follow-up meetings and final evaluation. These activities played an important developmental role in terms of keeping the initiative alive for sites, and introducing an external deadline for work. It seems important to acknowledge that using research interviews to influence the views and practice of participants is an inherent part of the process of doing development work such as this.

Finally, feedback to the training showed that it was successful and well-received by all the sites and that it provided a real, working model of user involvement in action. This, in itself, appeared to be responsible for significant changes in the attitudes and practices of the practitioners and people with learning difficulties who attended. The training days also provided time out for practitioners and people with learning difficulties to develop relationships and reach shared understanding of the concepts and commitment involved in implementing user involvement in staff recruitment.

How useful was the project as a format for promoting user involvement in staff recruitment?

Evidence from the project demonstrated that the structure of the four-step model was crucial in enabling participants to develop successful initiatives. The combination of opportunities to meet, talk, learn, practise, reflect and assess enabled some participants to make significant changes to their policy and practice. For example, many positive and important changes were apparent as a direct result of the sites' participation in the training programme (step 3). Other, smaller, changes to individuals' attitudes and assumptions occurred during the introductory meetings and presentations (step 1) or during the pre-training audit and goal-setting stages (step 2). However, the most significant and sustained changes were the result of work conducted during step 4, when sites developed their own initiatives for user involvement in recruitment, with support and evaluation from the project team.

By the end of the project, four of the five sites had developed detailed plans for initiatives to promote user involvement in staff recruitment, and three sites had implemented their plans at policy and/or practice level. The final section of this report summarises the main factors that appeared to be responsible for bringing about changes to policy and practice in the sites with which we worked with.

Strategies for promoting change and improving practice: a checklist

This report has shown how project participants used a number of different strategies to promote change and develop their practice around the issue of user involvement in choosing staff. We grouped these strategies under five main themes:

1. Commitment and attitudes
2. Working together
3. Organising resources
4. Developing skills and knowledge
5. Evaluating the process.

The ways in which sites attended to these themes had an impact on the extent to which they developed and implemented

initiatives for user involvement in recruitment. The most successful initiatives were developed by those sites which paid attention to all five themes and developed strategies to get the most value out of their involvement in the 'Learning to choose staff' project.

Our description of these themes and strategies is based on the evidence-base provided by the 'Learning to choose staff' project. However we believe that these messages have wider relevance. Both the model of the project itself, and the strategies developed by participants could be used to inform a range of other projects or initiatives. In particular, projects that aim to increase participation in practice and policy by people who use services would benefit from paying attention to some of the issues faced, and strategies developed by participants in the 'Learning to choose staff' project. The messages are also applicable to researchers who want to find ways to get their findings into practice.

With this in mind, we conclude with a general checklist of strategies for success in promoting change and improving practice.

Commitment and attitudes

- identify and/or develop champions and other key people to take the initiative forward and support them as appropriate;
- find champions at policy and practice levels;
- respond to different levels of commitment and challenge attitudes where necessary;
- define the extent and nature of commitment;
- record commitment to take part in the project, and to the underlying principles of the project;
- promote the role of people with learning difficulties as central to the success of the initiative;
- use evidence of success to promote and maintain commitment.

Working together

- identify key contacts at each site;
- identify other participants from the four stakeholder groups: people with learning difficulties, policy makers, managers, support staff;
- get agreement to take part;
- develop rapport and close working with key contacts;
- keep the perspective of people with learning difficulties at the forefront;
- establish, develop and maintain relationships within and between groups;
- find ways for practitioners and people with learning difficulties to work together on concrete tasks;
- include people with learning difficulties in meetings to discuss the project and initiatives where possible;
- find ways to keep the initiative alive.

Organising resources

- respond to the advice of key contacts and their working styles;
- plan and develop an initiative which includes opportunities to meet, talk, learn, practise, reflect and assess;
- set realistic and achievable goals including details of who will do what by when;
- provide support for those involved, especially people with learning difficulties;
- maintain flexibility;
- respond to challenges as they arise.

Developing skills and knowledge

- disseminate key findings about the topic/ initiative and its value;
- share information across stakeholder groups;
- recognise and value one another's abilities, needs and perspectives;
- ensure shared understanding of concepts;
- model good practice – plan an initiative where service users and practitioners learn and work together at each step;
- keep learning up to date;
- provide opportunities for putting learning into practice.

Evaluating the process

- document ongoing work and share this with others, including those 'outside' the initiative;
- provide opportunities to reflect on current practice, obstacles and opportunities;
- provide opportunities to set goals and develop action plans;
- evaluate progress against action plans/ goals;
- revise plans, and wider organisational practice, if necessary
- agree a date to feed back outcomes to everyone.

The final item on this list – agree a date to feed back outcomes to everyone – was added six months after we finished working with sites. We held a project conference to which all participants were invited, with 90 people attending on the day. It was a chance for the project team to provide overall feedback on the progress of the work, and for participants to exchange information both within and between their respective organisations. In addition, the conference was a celebration of people's hard work and involvement in the project, whatever the outcomes at that point. We hoped that it would act as a spur to further action and development for those sites that had not yet implemented their plans.

References

Gear, S., Graham, M., Howarth, J., Townsley, R. and Le Grys, P. (2000) *Images for equality*, Brighton: Pavilion.

Howarth, J., Graham, M. and Townsley, R. (2000) 'Head, heart, and hands. How people can choose their own staff', *Community Living*, vol 13, no 4, pp 12-13.

Kirk, S. (1996) 'Developing, disseminating and using research information', in M. Baker and S. Kirk (eds), *Research and development for the NHS: Evidence, evaluation and effectiveness*, Oxford: Radcliffe Medical Press.

Sloper, P., Mukherjee, S., Beresford, B., Lightfoot, J. and Norris, P. (1999) *Real change not rhetoric. Putting research into practice in multi-agency services*, Bristol: The Policy Press.

Townsley, R. and Macadam, M. (1996) *Choosing staff. The involvement of people with learning difficulties in staff recruitment*, Bristol: The Policy Press.

Townsley, R., Howarth, J., LeGrys, P. and Macadam, M. (1997) *Getting involved in choosing staff*, Brighton: Pavilion.

Appendix A:
Project Advisory Groups

We established two advisory groups to oversee the project as a whole. The Research Advisory Group comprised practitioners, researchers, trainers and consultants with an interest in the involvement of people with learning difficulties in staff recruitment. The Service User Advisory Group consisted of people with learning difficulties who had an interest in, or experience of staff selection within their home, place of work, or day service.

The Service User Advisory Group (SUAG) met monthly over the lifetime of the project. It was facilitated by Pete Le Grys, who also recruited its members. The role of the group was to:

- advise the project team on issues relating to staff recruitment from the perspective of service users;
- act as a 'test bed' and help to develop accessible materials about the project (eg a leaflet to explain the project, a tape and CD for people with learning difficulties summarising the main findings);
- contribute to the project in other practical ways (eg conducting interviews).

The SUAG played an important role in developing accessible project outputs. They commented on the text for the project leaflet, and developed a set of illustrations in collaboration with an illustrator. They also spent several sessions planning and developing ideas about the format of the project's findings for service users. This product was an audio tape and CD for people with learning difficulties based on interviews with service users as part of the final evaluation.

Discussions between the project team and the SUAG led to the suggestion that the SUAG might themselves conduct the final interviews on behalf of the project. The group recognised that they needed some training in research interview skills first, and thus commissioned a local 'self advocacy research group' to carry out a workshop on this issue. The SUAG conducted seven group interviews across the five sites, and the tape-recorded data informed both the final evaluation as well as the development of the accessible output for service users.

B

Appendix B: Outline of the training programme

This Appendix is a summary of the training programme we used with sites as part of the Learning to Choose Staff project. The summary is not intended as a detailed guide and should be read in conjunction with the other training materials available on this topic:

Townsley, R., Howarth, J., LeGrys, P. and Macadam, M. (1997) *Getting involved in choosing staff*, Brighton: Pavilion.

Gear, S., Graham, M., Howarth, J., Townsley, R., LeGrys, P. (2000) *Images for equality*, Brighton: Pavilion.

Day One – For people with learning difficulties and support staff

Objectives:
- To get to know each other
- To learn to work together
- To introduce the concept of the whole recruitment process
- To learn about person specifications and how to produce them
- To learn about advertisements and how to produce them

People and resources needed:
- Two trainers
- Support staff who work directly with people with learning difficulties (one support staff member for every four people with learning difficulties)
- People with learning difficulties who use the service
- Cushion
- Flipchart and pens
- Blutac
- Glue or sticky tape
- A set of 'recruitment pictures' to illustrate the main stages of the recruitment process. We made up a set of A4 sized cards, with hand-drawn pictures and labels for each of the following stages of recruitment: person specification, job description, adverts, information pack, short listing, interviewing, choosing.
- Job advertisements from newspapers and magazines.

Morning session

Introductions – Cushion throw
One person starts by holding the cushion and saying 'My name is ... and this is for ....' They then throw the cushion to the person they are addressing. This is

repeated until there is a sense of people knowing one another's names and feeling more relaxed.

Ground rules

These are gathered from the group and recorded on flipchart paper in pictures and words.

The whole recruitment process

- Explain that recruitment is about more than just doing interviews. Use the 'recruitment pictures' to illustrate this point.
- Split into smaller groups. Give each group some flipchart paper and one of the 'recruitment pictures'. Ask them to write/draw everything they know about this stage of the recruitment process. If they know nothing, that is fine – they are here to learn more. When they have put down everything they can think of, give them another picture until they have covered all the stages.
- Feedback from each group.
- Remind people that these different parts of the recruitment process are the things that will be covered during the training programme.

Break

Person specifications (1):
Bad worker, good worker

- Split into small groups – one support worker per group.
- Give each group coloured pens and a piece of flipchart with a large outline figure drawn on it.
- Ask each group to think about things that workers have done or said or looked like over the years that people have not liked. People may find this very difficult – it might mean remembering things from their past they would rather forget. Emphasise

that you don't need to know the names of workers who have done these things. Encourage people to think into their past, so that they are not expected to criticise current workers, as again many people find this hard to do. Encourage people to draw on the figure rather than write words.

- Acknowledge before moving on that this may have brought back painful/ difficult memories for some people.
- Give each group another sheet with an outline figure drawn on it. This time ask them to think of good workers – what do they do, say, look like that makes them good workers? It may be helpful to think of a worker they particularly like and say what they like about this person. Again encourage people to record their thoughts using drawings.
- Each group feedback to whole group about what they have done.

Person specifications (2):
Head, heart, hand

- Draw a head, heart and hand down the left-hand side of a piece of flipchart paper. Explain that a person specification is about what people need to know (head), what sort of person they are (heart) and what they need to be able to do (hand).
- Ask people to get back into their groups and draw their own head, heart on a piece of flipchart paper.
- Then ask them to look at their 'good worker' sheet and to transfer each phrase or point onto the 'head, heart, hand' sheet. For example the point 'can drive a car' would go by 'hand' as it relates to what a person should be able to do.
- Then ask groups to look at the 'bad worker' sheet and turn the phrases and points here into positive statements. For example, 'shouts' might become 'talks nicely to me'.

- Feedback to whole group.

Afternoon session

Cushion throw

Making job advertisements (1)
- Ask people to get into groups that are different from those they were in during the morning.
- Give each group copies of the job advertisements pages from newspapers and magazines.
- Ask them to look through and cut out anything they like the look of.
- Ask people to paste their chosen advertisements onto flipchart paper and talk about why they liked this particular example.
- If people can read ask them to look at what is on every advertisement, eg closing date, telephone number etc.
- Record all comments.

Making job advertisements (2)
- Give each group half a sheet of flipchart.
- Using all the above information ask them to make their own advertisements.
- Show everyone what they have done.

Summary
- Look at all the flip charts on the wall and remind people of what they have covered during the day.
- Look at the 'recruitment pictures' and explain what will be covered on Day Two.
- Ask people to bring photos of where they live or their day service for Day Two.

End of Day One

Day Two – For people with learning difficulties and support staff

Objectives:
- To continue to work together
- To learn about information packs and how to produce them
- To talk about equal opportunities issues, prejudice and discrimination
- To learn about, and practise, the short listing process

People and resources needed:
- Two trainers
- Support staff who work directly with people with learning difficulties (one support staff member for every four people with learning difficulties)
- People with learning difficulties who use the service
- Cushion
- Flipchart and pens
- A4 sized paper
- Blutac
- Glue or sticky tape
- Photos or pictures about the service and the people who live or work there
- 'Images for Equality' photo pack, or a range of photos representing people who could be disabled, young, old, gay or lesbian, or from black and minority ethnic groups.
- Three sets of 'statement cards' developed from the person specifications that people made on Day One. Set One should represent statements from the person specifications such as 'can do first aid', 'sorts out arguments', etc. Set Two should cover the opposites such as 'doesn't know about first aid', 'can't drive'. Set Three is a list of unrelated statements such as 'likes cats', or 'supports Manchester United'.

Morning session

Cushion throw

Review of Day One

Making an information pack about the service

- Ask the whole group to think about the sort of things that people need to know about the service that will help them decide if they want to apply for a job there. List these thoughts on a flipchart.
- Split into small groups, and ask people to make a pack based on the list generated above. They can use A4 paper, and the photos or pictures they have brought with them.
- Share the developing information packs with the whole group. People will probably need to carry this work on away from the training course.

Break

What is equal opportunities?

- Ask the whole group to think and talk about when they have not been treated fairly.
- Record people's ideas about 'what happened' on one piece of flipchart, and 'how they felt' on another.
- This can bring up strong emotions which need to be allowed expression!
- Explain that the things people have shared are examples of what happens when you are treated unfairly. But equal opportunities is about treating people fairly.

Afternoon session

Cushion throw

Discussing equal opportunities

You will need the 'Images for Equality' photo pack, or a set of at least 30 photographs representing people who could be disabled, young, old, gay or lesbian, or from black and minority ethnic groups.

- Reminder – How can we treat people fairly? How do we like to be treated?

Brief summary of the activity (please see the 'Images for Equality' pack for more details):

- Split into two groups, one trainer with each group.
- Using the photos ask 'how would you feel about this person coming to live/work with you?'
- Make sure everyone has a chance to have their say.
- Accept answers without judgement, and show you understand but you do not necessarily agree.
- Using participants' words clarify what it is they like/don't like about the person.
- Once enough views are gathered start to gently challenge prejudices. Eg:
  - How do you know they are good or bad?
  - What don't you like about the black woman?
- Continue to gently challenge.
- Use the photographs to discuss other prejudices that may not be based on appearance, such as sexual orientation, marital status, hidden impairments. For example, if people have said they like a particular person, tell them that this person is gay/lesbian, has three children, has epilepsy and so on. What do people feel about the person in the photograph now?

- Some of the photographs are of the same person in different styles of dress, facial expression etc. Use these to draw out other prejudices.
- End by reminding people about prejudice, what it is, and how it should not be used to form a judgement or acted upon.

Short-listing

- Devise a scoring system with the groups. This could be based on a tick-sheet; rating out of three, ten, etc; or using smiley/not smiley faces.
- Use the photographs from earlier (although photographs are not used in real short listing, it gives a chance to further challenge prejudice and embed equal opportunities). Take four photographs, two of people the group liked, two of people about whom they were less positive.
- On a flipchart list six important points from their person specifications, eg 'knows first aid', 'can sort out arguments'. These are now the short-listing criteria.
- Blutac the photos across the top of the flipchart.
- Allocate a selection of 'statement cards' from each of the three lists for each photo. These are fictional points from the person's 'application'.
- Ask people to score each person based on an analysis of their suitability against the short-listing criteria. Which two people would the group interview?
- Complete the activity by asking the group 'what more do we need to know about these people?' and 'how can we find these things out?' The answer is by doing interviews!

Summary and end of Day Two

Day Three – For people with learning difficulties and support staff

Objectives:
- To continue to work together
- To learn how to listen
- To prepare for an interview and practise interviewing candidates
- To learn about, and practise, the choosing process

People and resources needed:
- Two trainers
- Support staff who work directly with people with learning difficulties (one support staff member for every four people with learning difficulties)
- People with learning difficulties who use the service
- Cushion
- Flipchart and pens
- A4 sized paper
- Blutac
- Glue or sticky tape
- Person specifications developed on Day One.

Morning session

Cushion throw

Review of Day Two
Remind the group that we still need to find out more about people who might apply for a job in their service.

Learning to listen
- Trainers model good and bad listening (see 'Getting involved in choosing staff' for more on this).
- Whole group list the things that show we are listening.

Asking open and closed questions
- Explain open and closed questions (see 'Getting involved in choosing staff' for more on this).
- Identify who, what, where, when and how as good ways of asking questions.
- Identify some topics to ask questions about, such as favourite TV programmes, holidays, hobbies, etc.
- Ask people to get into pairs and decide who will be Person A and Person B.
- Person A asks a mixture of open and closed questions about the topic, whilst listening to the answers of Person B. Then each pair swap roles.
- Discuss this process as a group.

Break

Making questions for interview
- In small groups identify four to six items from the person specifications.
- Develop open questions to find out more about these things.
- Record the questions, in writing or pictures.

Preparing for interview
- Try out different ways of setting up the interview room.
- Develop a scoring system again
- Work out the supporter's role.

Afternoon session

Practising interviewing candidates
- Identify two 'candidates' for interview. The candidates could be members of support staff or one or both of the trainers.
- Allocate each candidate role of either 'good' worker or 'not so good' worker.
- Practise the interviews, using the questions developed above
- Give candidates a score, using the scoring system developed above.

Choosing who gets the job
- With reference to the scoring system, discuss who was the best person for the job.
- Prepare some feedback for both candidates and give this to them.
- Talk about what people have learnt from preparing and practising the interview process.

Summary
- Look back over the last three days' work, using the various materials and flipcharts that have been created.
- Talk about working with the bosses (managers and policy makers). Explain what is going to happen and get commitment from people with learning difficulties to attend Days Four and Five.
- Organise travel and support arrangements for Days Four and Five.

End of Day Three

Days Four and Five – For people with learning difficulties and managers (for Day Four) or policy makers (for Day Five)

Objectives:
- To get to know each other
- To learn to work together
- To find ways to progress the involvement of people with learning difficulties in staff recruitment within the service

People and resources needed:
- Two trainers
- People with learning difficulties who use the service and who attended Days One to Three
- Managers (Day Four), or policy makers (Day Five)

- Cushion
- Flipchart and pens
- Blutac
- Glue or sticky tape

Morning session

Introductions – Cushion throw

Good worker, bad worker
- Do a shortened version of this activity with mixed groups of service users and managers/policy makers.
- Trainers circulate to model good interaction and facilitate.

Head, heart, hands
- Again a shortened version of this activity.
- Again trainers facilitate and model good interaction.

Break

What do people want?
- Mixed small groups of people with learning difficulties and managers/policy makers to discuss 'what involvement do people with learning difficulties want in the recruitment process?'
- Feedback to whole group

Afternoon session

Reactions to working together
- What feelings and thoughts did the managers/policy makers have from the morning session?

Obstacles and opportunities
- Explain 'force field analysis' – that there is a central aim, such as the involvement of people with learning difficulties in staff recruitment. That there are forces that enable people to

work towards the central aim, such as 'the time is right', or 'people want more involvement'. These are opportunities. But there are also forces pulling away from the aim to prevent it happening, such as 'too difficult', or 'personnel won't let it happen' etc. These are obstacles.
- With the whole group, identify obstacles and opportunities in relation to the central aim. Write these on a flipchart.
- Ask people to get into small groups and choose one or two obstacles and opportunities. How can they make the most of the opportunities? How can they reduce the obstacles?
- Feed back and share thoughts and ideas with the whole group.

Break

Action planning
- Ask people to identify the next steps.
- How can they put their ideas and learning into practice?
- Who is going to do what? By when?
- Agree an action plan for the service as a whole.

End of Day Four or Five